SEDITIOUS THINGS

THE SONGS OF JOSEPH MATHER-SHEFFIELD'S GEORGIAN PUNK POET

1889books

Seditious Things:

The Songs of Joseph Mather-Sheffield's Georgian Punk Poet

Published 2017 by 1889 books

Cover, 2017 introduction, and map: copyright © Steven R Kay
2017, 1889 books

Front cover font: "Shortcut." Courtesy of Eduardo Recife.
© Eduardo Recife/Misprinted Type
[http://www.misprintedtype.com]

Back cover text: "Belligerent Madness" copyright © 2008 by P.D. Magnus/Fontmonkey

www.1889books.co.uk

ISBN: 978-0-9935762-4-9

*Facts are seditious things
When they touch courts and kings*

CONTENTS

Introduction to this 2017 Edition   1

1862 Edition:
    Preface to the Reader   14
    Memoir of Joseph Mather   16
    Introduction   20

Preface to the 1811 Edition   36

The Songs of Joseph Mather:

The File Hewer's Lamentation	37
Author's Petition to Fortune	38
Mr. Batty's Mule	40
Bad Luck to the Crow and the Owl	41
Spence Broughton's Lament	44
Buggy Eyre	45
Nell and Jos	47
Timber Legg'd Harry	48
Sheffield Races	49
Ditto, Part Second	50
Jezebel's Daughter	52
Ditto, Part Second	54
John Oldham's Disaster	56
Ben Eyre	58
Frank Fearne	59
Loxley Edge	60
Stevens and Lastley's Execution	62
The Derbyshire Farmer	63
The Castigation	65
Fish and Tommy Ticktack	66
Dr. Kelly	68
The Hen-pecked Husband	70
The Crookes Rogue	72
Nell and the Journeyman Hatter	72
Hallamshire Haman	74

Sancho	77
Britons Awake	79
True Reformers	81
Norfolk Street Riots	83
The Brawn	87
Elegy on R. Clay, Esq.,	88
The Black Resurrection	90
Raddle-necked Tups	93
Nothing like leather	96
The Cock-tail Lady	98
Shoutemdown's Barm	100
The Blind Fiddlers	103
God Save Great Thomas Paine	105
The Guinea Club Feast	107
The Nether Green Lad	108
The Justass	109
The Owl's Commission	111
He's out of Commission, Boys	111
Watkinson and his Thirteens	113
Bang Beggar	117
Watkinson's Repentance	119
Tape Allen	120
The Thanksgiving	120
Repentance	122
The Royal George	124
The Valentine	125
The Cock-tail Feast	127
Ditto, Part Second	130
Round-Legs to Wadsley went	133
The Face Card	136
The Rimsey Old Man	138

Songs not in the 1862 edition:

The Standard of Freedom	140
Her Master's Bed	141
Sheffield the Black	143
Hey Turk	144

Miscellaneous Songs from the 1862 edition:

Saturday Night	144
The Jovial Cutlers	147
The Cutler's Song	150
The Cutlin' Heroes	152
Rotherham Fair	154
The Mayor of Donchester	157
The Volunteer	164
The Quack Doctor	167
A Song in the Yorkshire Dialect	168
Mr. Bourne and his Wife	170
Tom Topsail	171
The Trip Match	173
The Grinders' Hardships	174
Dr. Shinar's the Lad for the Ladies	176
Poor Robin	178
The Funeral	179
Rotherham Statutes	182

Map of Sheffield in the 1780s 185

Memorial to those re-interred from St Pauls 186

INTRODUCTION TO THE 2017 EDITION

Joseph Mather is a giant of Sheffield history and yet his name is unfamiliar to most Sheffielders today. We hope by this volume to redress that—at least a bit. Mather did something truly special in his time in articulating and communicating the problems of ordinary people and the injustices of the society he lived in. Despite the passage of the years since he died in 1804, and progress in many areas, if he were alive today Mather would still be railing against inequalities, and would recognise the Tories of today as broadly the same species he knew back then.

You will find no statues to one of the greatest Sheffielders in history, no plaques—not even a gravestone—this was disposed of without ceremony when St Paul's was demolished and his remains scooped up with others and dumped in a common grave in Abbey Lane cemetery in the 1930s. His memory was quietly buried too by the city's middle classes, and gradually his memory through oral tradition amongst the ordinary folk of the town has been lost.

His verse has largely been dismissed as "merest doggerel"[1] and therefore was not celebrated by worthy Sheffielders like the works of Ebenezer Elliott. But that is to misunderstand completely what Mather achieved. His verse was not for reading in drawing rooms but for singing in the pubs and taverns. That is why we wanted not just to produce a book, but to hear it brought properly to life in song. His was irreverent anti-establishment street art. For a 2016 *Festival of the Mind* project Ray Hearne showed just how good Mather's songs were when he performed them live in Barker's Pool. A CD of the recordings is included in some editions of this book, and is available to buy online.

To understand Mather today you have to first understand a little about the Sheffield he lived in: his songs chronicle key events of those times. When he was born in 1737, Sheffield was a town of about 10,000 citizens and was expanding rapidly as manufacturing advances such as crucible steel and silver plate made Sheffield wares desirable. At the same time changes in agriculture including the Enclosures Acts drove working people to the towns. Advances in transport by road, the navigability of the Don, and more efficient

---

[1] Sheffield historian Mary Walton

banking lead to further expansion.

Conditions for common people in the town were far from sanitary with no drainage or running water, housing then being little more than hovels. Mather himself was, according to Wilson, born in "Cack Alley," a jennel off West Bar Green, though other (unverifiable) sources say he was one of the immigrants coming from the countryside: Chelmorton, near Buxton, in Derbyshire. By 1792 the population of the town had risen to around 40,000.

Mather was apprenticed to the trade of file-cutting in the workshop of Nicholas Jackson in the 1750s — and if *The File-Hewer's Lamentation* is as autobiographical as is supposed, set up as a "little mester" himself at one stage. It was not unusual for those in the trade to drift in and out of direct employment to "self-employed" freeman status as their circumstances changed.

The events of the American War, 1775 to 1783, and its aftermath had a significant bearing on the political climate in Sheffield. Trade stagnated as Sheffield had become highly dependent on the American market; what pioneer in the New World would not want a quality knife? This inevitably brought hardship. Strikes for better wages in 1777 and 1787 in the file, table-knife, scissor and spring-knife industries were partially successful but by the strike of 1794 the tables had turned.

Power began to be concentrated in the hands of the merchant classes and large manufacturers, to the detriment of the freemen cutlers ('little mesters') and journeymen (hired hands). The huge polarisation of capital and labour had begun. The Cutlers' Company previously had been seen as a defender of the rights of the "property of labour" – there was a degree of democracy which evened out the divisions between masters and men. The 1780s saw a bitter fight for the soul of the Company which ended in its emasculation and decline into little more than an excuse for a lavish dinner for the town's wealthy. The power of money won – but left behind was a strongly politicised underclass, which had gained experience of organising.

Other events served to raise people's sense of injustice. The song *Stevens and Lastley's Execution* recounts a notable event: these two were executed in April 1790 for what was believed to be little more than a Saturday night, post-tavern prank gone wrong. The constable George Eyre (see: *Buggy Eyre*) and the local magistrate James Wilkinson reacted over-zealously – whether the two "miscreants" were known local radicals can only be guessed at. However, the arrests coincided with a visit by the Prince of Wales and the Duke of Norfolk to Wentworth Woodhouse, the home of the nearest local aristocrat, Earl Fitzwilliam. Was Wilkinson, who was not known for being a harsh man, trying to show he was in control of the town in advance of his invitation to the ball in the Prince's honour?

The approach of the end of the 18th century saw great upheaval in Europe, and Sheffield was not immune from this. By 1790, fear of Jacobinism led to the law being used against strikes — five of the leaders of the scissor grinders' strike were imprisoned in Wakefield in September 1790.

The strike started in late Spring that year when Jonathan Watkinson, a master scissor smith, announced that he was changing the terms on which he contracted out grinding. The long-accepted tradition was for fourteen blades to be sent out and, accepting that sometimes one or two were substandard, the expectation was for only twelve to be returned and paid for. This also allowed some leeway for "perks of the trade" – any that weren't broken being sold on. *Watkinson and his Thirteens* refers to his change to sending out only thirteen and expecting twelve to be returned: an effective pay cut.

The song *Hallamshire Haman* is about George Wood, a scissor manufacturer and Senior Warden of the Cutlers' Company, seen as responsible for the prosecution of the strike leaders. The song is based on the story from the Old Testament of Haman and Mordecai – where Haman fails to destroy Mordecai so instead vows to destroy all his people, the Jews.

In 1791 there were demonstrations against widespread enclosure around Sheffield including further enclosure of Crookes Moor — which had been the site of Sheffield races (the course running from the modern day Broomhill along Fulwood Road).

The main landowning beneficiaries were to be the Duke of Norfolk, the principal landowner in the town, and the Vicar of Sheffield, the Rev. Wilkinson. (In a sense, it could be said that the philanthropy of a later Duke of Norfolk in creating a park for the citizens of the town, was little more than repairing some of the damage done by his predecessor. Also, interestingly, tens of thousands of Sheffielders still pay ground rent to the current Duke of Norfolk, a further relic of this land-grab.)

The commons were also used for bare-knuckle fights, outdoor leisure for the working classes and grazing for their animals. This enclosure provoked a reaction that earlier enclosures had not, presumably because of the popularity of the amenities and the growing politicisation. Against these anti-enclosure demonstrators, troops were dispatched from Nottingham, in itself a very provocative act: strong-arm tactics from outsiders having echoes of Orgreave down the centuries. People then responded by attacking, in turn, the prison (with a nod to the Bastille?), and the property of the Enclosures Commissioners: Vicar Wilkinson's Broom Hall and of Vincent Eyre, the Duke of Norfolk's agent. Doubtless, recent memories of Wilkinson – the "old serpent," the "black diabolical fiend" – for his role in the in the "Black Resurrection" and the executions of Stevens and Lastley were also on people's minds. More soldiers were sent from York to restore order, and a "rioter," and probable scapegoat, John Bennett, was hanged.

The Rights of Man by Thomas Paine was by then in wide circulation. Every cutler was said to have a copy. This publication was regarded by the establishment as dangerous and was banned as seditious libel, and Paine outlawed. The song *Britons Awake* was written in response to this assault.

After the execution of Louis XVI, and the declaration of war against France — something which was widely condemned in Sheffield for its damaging effect on trade, as well as from principle — the Sheffield Constitutional Society (which emerged from the disputes of ordinary cutlers with the Cutlers' Company) wrote: "We have many thousand members, but a vast majority of them being working Men, the war, which has deprived many of the them of *all* employment, and almost every one of *half* his earnings, we have been crippled more than any other in the kingdom. —We have the satisfaction to know that we have done great good, but I fear we must content ourselves with good intentions and wishes in the future, as our funds are not only exhausted, but the society is considerably in debt…"[2]

Sheffield's reformist tendencies flourished for several reasons — reasons which may still have echoes through to today. Firstly, it had little aristocratic influence and no great civil power: its two magistrates in 1792 living out of town. It had many "little mesters" — highly skilled and well-paid craftsman — often literate, who cherished their independence. Joseph Mather was one such — able to read if not write. They were also well organised and easily formed associations. There were several factors in this: firstly they had gained experience during disputes with the Cutlers' Company, and secondly Sheffield had a high proportion of religious dissenters – they had grievances resulting from the Test and Corporations Act, restricting their ability to hold certain official positions, and crucially they were used to organising through the structures of their chapels. Reformers also had a weekly newspaper *The Sheffield Register* under the editorship of Joseph Gales who supported the Constitutional Society and spread its message. The newspaper was founded in 1787 and by 1794 had a circulation of around 2000, and was one of the most effective provincial newspapers of its day, giving a lot of space to local issues and opinion. Gales also may have made the acquaintance of Paine when he stayed near Sheffield, but this point is uncertain, though he certainly had many contacts amongst reformers across the country. To this you must add Sheffield's "tavern-culture" – proving spaces for reading newspapers aloud, debating and the singing of songs.

Events in France and Europe hit Sheffield trade hard — denying access to markets that had opened up with the continent. Sheffielders were energised by all this change. There was a lot of support for the French Revolution in the town. An assessment of the disposition of troops was made by the Secretary of War's Deputy Adjutant-General, Colonel De Lancey, in June 1792. You can almost hear him foaming at the mouth here: at Sheffield he 'found that seditious doctrines of Paine and the factious people who are endeavouring to disturb the peace of the country had extended to a degree very much beyond my conception.' He reported that: 'as the wages given to the journeymen are very high, it is pretty

---

[2] Appendix C to the second report from the House of Commons Committee of Secrecy (1794) – online: archive.org

generally the practice for them to work for three days, in which they can earn sufficient to enable them to drink and riot for the rest of the week. Consequently no place can be more fit for seditious purposes.' Two thousand five hundred 'of the lowest mechanics' were enrolled in the principal reform association (the Constitutional Society): 'Here they read the most violent publications, and comment on them, as well as on their correspondence not only with the dependent societies in the towns and villages in the vicinity, but with those in other parts of the kingdom…'

Such seditious machinations included things like collecting 10,000 signatures on a petition to Parliament demanding, of all things, universal male suffrage. At the time Sheffielders had no direct representation whatsoever in Parliament and didn't until 1832 (other than freeholders able to travel to York to vote, who had a say in Yorkshire's two MPs).

November 1792 saw the town celebrate the successes of the French army against Austria and Prussia at Valmy — a procession of five or six thousand drew a quartered ox through the streets amid the firing of cannon, the wearing of red liberty caps and the flying of the French flag. In the procession was a caricature painting representing Britannia — Edmund Burke riding a swine — an allusion to Burke's condemnation of the French Revolution in his 1790 publication and the contempt he revealed for ordinary people in his reference to the "swinish multitude."

The clampdown was draconian as the propertied classes and aristocracy took fear, especially given the turn of events in France as the aristocracy were put to the sword.

This no doubt hastened the construction of a barracks in the town the following year for two hundred cavalrymen.

Mather's song *True Reformers* relates to a scandalous event in this period in British history as the ruling classes wielded their iron fist in a very British, judicial way. As the law stood in 1793 in England, the ruling classes had a dilemma when it came to strangling reform: they could indict someone for high treason or the lesser charge of seditious libel – but both of these handed the powers to the vagaries of the jury. The only other course was summary trial on lesser charges by local magistrates. None of these were sufficiently robust or reliable to strike the sort of terror into dissenters needed to kill off the movement. Scottish law, however, was different: judges were more pliable and juries could be selected. The authorities arrested and prosecuted Thomas Muir, a gifted Scottish leader who was transported for 14 years by what we would now call a kangaroo court. This was followed by the trial of the Rev. Thomas Fyshe Palmer, whose crime was that of writing an address against the war. He was sent to Botany Bay for 7 years. Scottish reformers refused to be cowed and in November 1793 a National Convention was called, to which English reformers were invited. In a show of solidarity delegates were sent: Matthew Browne from Sheffield; with Thomas Hardy, Joseph Gerrald and Maurice Margarot attending for London. The Scottish secretary of the Friends of the People was William Skirving. More trials followed: of Skirving and Margarot who received 14 years transportation, then of Gerrald whose weak health meant that transportation was a death sentence. Skirving also died within a year of arrival in New South Wales. (The sacrifice of these men should be remembered by people who say they can't be bothered to vote in the 21st century.)

Government launched further assaults on the Constitutional Societies: the Sheffield delegate, Matthew Campbell Browne, was arrested. Then in April 1794, at Castle Hill in Sheffield, 10,000-12,000 protesters against the Scottish sentences gathered at an open-air meeting. It was chaired by the powerful orator, and National Convention delegate, Henry Yorke, who gave a two-hour long address in favour of universal rights. There followed trials of Hardy and Yorke; and it was in this atmosphere that Joseph Gales, radical editor of *The Sheffield Register* was indicted for conspiracy and fled to America. Legislation was further tightened with the Seditious Meetings Act of 1797 which banned the holding of meetings and the Combinations Act of 1799 which outlawed trades unions. Today's Tory party may be more subtle, but their 2016 Trade Union Bill shows how little their hatred of the rights of association has abated.

This was the climate into which Mather, with his abilities as a songsmith, was thrust, and the period through which his songs give an alternative commentary. He was able to communicate ideas and passions to ordinary people — the classes incapable of reading *The*

Register or *The Rights of Man*. He was one of their own, and he was an entertainer: with his hallmark of singing off the back of a donkey, or bull, backwards. This was the 18th century equivalent of the jukebox, karaoke, or stand-up.

Joseph Mather's talent was natural – he had no education beyond his ability to read, and if he could write at all it was very badly. One of his friends was a young man called Arthur Jewitt[3], the son of one of the leaders of the dispute between the freemen cutlers and the Cutlers' Company. Jewitt says of Mather: "he was however really and truly a poet and for forcible expressions in any think {sic} satirical or plaintive I have never seen his superior. With education it is difficult to say what he might have been."

Mather composed his songs at his workbench, wielding his six pound hammer. He would arrange them line by line in his mind and commit them to memory. (You can imagine the hammer marking out the rhythm as he worked.) Then he would get one of his fellow workmen to write them down "on a slate or sheet of shabby paper."

Jewitt then describes how Mather would often bring them to him to correct the spellings before taking them to be printed by the radical printer John Crome in Campo Lane. He says that the dispute with the Cutlers' Company was for Mather a prolific time: "it was not to be expected that Joseph Mather would let his mind be idle particularly when he was one of those who felt most interested in the event – he therefore gave his Pegasus a loose rein and composed song after song satirizing some or other of the opposite party."

Mather performed in the streets at the end of the week, after payday, when people were out doing their market shopping – and supping. He went round the taverns and seasonal festivals, fairs and race-weeks. Back then Sheffield had a race-week where he was a regular 'turn,' until Crookes Moor was taken from the people and enclosed in the earlier 1779 enclosures. He would have sold his printed songs as he went.

Audience participation would have been a necessity — the tunes chosen were often popular ones from chapel. In the Hallamshire Haman the last word "hell" was often missed and instead of being vocalised was replaced by rapping on tables.

---

[3] Jewitt's unpublished memoir is held by Wigan Archives in the Edward Hall Collection: "Passages in the life of A E Jewitt."

Ray Hearne reckons that Mather would have "heard, adapted, borrowed, chopped, changed and tailored the tunes and melodies that he heard from other singers, either local or passers through. That for me is how the people's tradition has always worked. It's mucky, grubby from pawing by innumerable gentle and powerful dirty hands; a vibrant, dynamic and exquisite vehicle capable of transmitting as great an artistic experience as any other art form Radio Three might mention."

Another interesting aspect of Mather's story is that he was never put on trial for his views (it seems his only time in gaol was for his debts). Was he dismissed as irrelevant, or over-looked by the authorities? This seems unlikely given the penetration of the barbs. One factor as provided by Jewitt was that: "though they [Mather's 'effusions' printed by Crome] were highly libellous, and the parties attached sought out for evidence so that they might prosecute the printer the wary Scotchman [Crome] denied their attempts by always taking care to have his types disturbed before a single copy left his office." Another factor is perhaps as Winifred Gales (Joseph's wife) said, to explain why it was so long before they came for her husband, that: "we lived in Sheffield, in the hearts of the people, who would have risen en masse at any intemperate proceedings – two-thirds of the people would not inform – the rest dare not." You can imagine no-one ever knowing, when questioned, where the songs came from and denying that they had ever purchased any, never mind who the author was.

Wilson said that little was known of Mather's parentage or of his early history. The same applies today. In fact not much trace of him exists in the historical record except for his songs and what can be gleaned from them. His passing was noted briefly in the Iris in the "Died" column: "A few days ago Mr Joseph Mather, formerly a well-known character in this town." The fact that his gravestone and remains were treated with irreverence would have caused him to turn in his grave (had he still got one): in the *Black Resurrection* he rails against the trashing of the graveyard around St Peter's when Church Lane was widened into what is now Church Street.

Chronology

1737 Mather's birth
1750s Mather apprenticed as a file-cutter
1775-1783 American War
1782 Execution of Frank Fearne
1784-1791 Disputes over the Act of Incorporation of the Cutlers' Company
1787 First edition of *The Register*
1789 Start of the French Revolution
1790 (March) Execution of Stevens and Lastley
1790 (summer) – scissor grinders' strike
1791 (July) Sheffield Crookesmoor Enclosures Riots
1791 (March) First part of *The Rights of Man* published, extracts published in *The Register* that summer
1791 (August) French Declaration of Rights and Constitution printed in *The Register*
1791 (December) Founding of the Sheffield Association for Constitutional Information (later the Sheffield Constitutional Society, then the Sheffield Society for Constitutional Information)
1792 (January) Cheap edition of *The Rights of Man* published in Sheffield, followed by the publication of the second part in February
1792 (April) Spence Broughton executed
1792 (May) Royal proclamation against seditious writing – urging magistrates to use existing powers to bring prosecutions
1792 (July) Construction starts on a new barracks for 200 cavalry at a site off the current Infirmary Road (Barrack Lane named after this) (completed 1794)
1792 (September) storming of the Tuileries
1792 (November) Celebration of French Victory at Valmy, Sheffield's address to the National Convention in Paris
1792 (December) Thomas Paine outlawed, *The Rights of Man* condemned as seditious libel
1793 (January) Execution of Louis XVI
1793 (February) France declares war against Britain and Holland
1793 (November) Edinburgh Convention: "Friends of the People"
1794 (April) Mass meeting on Castle Hill
1794 (May) Suspension of Habeas Corpus
1794 (August) Joseph Gales' exile

1795 (August) Norfolk Street Riot
1804 Mather's death

<u>Collecting Mather's Songs</u>

Mather's songs were not printed until probably the 1780s when some were distributed as "broadsides" on flimsy paper and sold for a penny or a ha'penny. Such printed ballads were the most widely available reading material amongst the poor at the time. They therefore played an important part in influencing opinion and educating people about how government oppressed them, and of the need for reform.

It is not known if any of these original printed ballads still exist. There are photocopies of two in Sheffield local studies Library (from one of which the copy of the woodcut of Watkinson was taken – song XLIV); however, they are not to be found in Sheffield Archives. If anyone can help with this, please let us know.

It is entirely possible that Mather was not the author of some of these songs. Jewitt claims that he wrote some songs satirizing the Freemen's opponents which were printed by Crome and attributed to Mather. Mather apparently declaring: "of some of these that he knew not whose was the child but he was at no loss to know who would be considered its father." We consider him the father of all the songs here.

The first collection of the songs was published in 1811, by John Crome. In that book, he put out an appeal for songs which he knew to exist in written form but which he was unable to obtain for that volume. These named songs were: Bloodhounds and Snap, Riots at Coalyard, Tom Pox'em, His Son Joe's Breeches, Robin Lighthead, Dampey's Journey to Grimesthorpe, Young Johnny's Nightcap, Spring Gardens, Wilkes and Liberty, Rats Subdued by the Mice, Mrs Frazer, Killamarsh Forge, Solomon had a pig of his own, Young Sorrel, David Kilner, Rough Robin from Curbar, Captain Colley, Wanton Tommy, Black Game of Cribbage, Tommy Kenney's Club Rules. Should anyone stumble across any of these in their attic, please get in touch.

Crome may have produced another version in 1823, though we have been unable to trace a copy of that.

The song we have called *Her Master's Bed* is taken from the 1811 edition.

It was in 1862 that John Wilson published his remarkable work, which forms the main base of this 2017 volume.

In addition the songs 'The Standard of Freedom' and 'Sheffield the Black' have been added. The former was reproduced in a 1970s Holberry Society Bulletin, the latter was posted on the Sheffield History website by John Mather (no relation) and was sent him by historian Eric Youle. Beyond that the authorship cannot currently be proved.

We have added *Hey Turk* – there is reference to it and a version of the chorus in the footnote to the song Ben Eyre. These verses were taken from R.E. Leader's 1876 *Reminiscences of Old Sheffield*. That book implies some doubt as to who wrote it, but given Wilson's note it seems compelling enough to include it. *Reminiscences* has two additional verses which don't seem connected, so have been omitted.

Wilson also added some other local folk songs to his volume and, although not attributed to Mather, we have left them in this edition. Two of these: *The Mayor of Donchester*, and *To a Robin Redbreast* are the work of James Montgomery.

John Wilson was an admirer of Mather from a distance in time. He treads carefully, given the changes in society and ideas of morality during the intervening period, and often ends up apologising for Mather's coarseness: the moral faults of Mather needing to be forgiven as being common to the age — how Victorian society had become more civilized and looking back on predecessors with a certain filter of moral superiority. That he couldn't bring himself to publish *Her Master's Bed* speaks volumes. However, Wilson's collection was a remarkable piece of amateur scholarship — providing explanation and background notes. He also gives each song a title, most of which were the names they are likely to have been known by. Wilson excuses any error by saying: "the only apology I can offer for any defects of mine is that the work has been accomplished in moments stolen from my slumbers. The cares of a family would not allow me to devote time which duty required to be devoted to more *profitable* pursuit. Should the work prove either amusing or instructing to any class of the community, the labour bestowed will not be regretted." We shake hands across the generations with Wilson. The same excuse applies to the publisher of this edition. We don't expect it to provide any real return on the time invested (…no expectation of either literary honours or emoluments!) We just hope to restore at least a little of Mather's rightful position as a great Sheffielder.

Note on the text:

John Wilson said: "The annotations to the songs might have been rendered more pungent by revealing the names of some of the persons introduced by Mather. The editor, however, has no desire to obtain *popularity* by causing *pain* to innocent parties." Wilson also abbreviated profanities. We have taken the position of trying to re-insert names and profanities wherever we could.

Steven Kay and Jack Windle, 2017

PREFACE TO THE READER (1862)

In issuing to the public this volume of local songs, the editor has no expectation of obtaining either literary honours or emoluments. His connection with the book is the result of accident. For the coarse language he is not responsible—no one being more fully aware of Mather's defects than his present editor. But as "Old Chaucer" says:

[4]"Who so shall telle a tale after a man,
 He moste reherse as neighe as ever he can
"Eyerich word, if it be in his charge;
"All, speke he never so rudely and so large;
"Or elles he moste tellen his tale *untrewe,*
"Or feinen thinges or finden words new.
"He may not spare although he were his brother;
"He moste as wel sayn O word as an other.
"Crist spoke himself ful brode in holy writ,
"And wel he wrote no vilanie is it;
"Eke Plato sayeth, who so can him rede,
"The wordes wrote Ben Cosin to the dede."

Therefore having no desire to "feinen thinges," or give to these songs a fictitious character, all their defects must be placed to the faults of the age in which they were written. Some of the songs are historically interesting, showing, as they do, the state of feeling that existed between masters and workmen in a bygone age. Others have never before been printed, and in obtaining such from oral tradition some defects may have occurred. The same remarks will apply to many of the notes, tradition being the only source from which information was obtainable. The annotations to the songs might have been rendered more pungent by revealing the names of some of the persons introduced by Mather. The editor, however, has no desire to obtain *popularity* by causing *pain* to innocent parties. Supposing all that was sung of them be true, the present generation are not responsible for ancestral sins. Some of the songs will be interesting to the politician, others to the artizan, while some will perhaps excite the attention of the archaeologist in his inquiries

---

[4] Prologue, Canterbury Tales.

after old things. Many of the notes which are added are only amplifications of some which were written for my own amusement as marginal references to a manuscript copy of songs which I had collected. If the original editor of Mather found difficulties in his path, the lapse of more than half a century has not lessened them. Several of the "Miscellaneous Songs" which have never before been printed, I thought sufficiently interesting to rescue from oblivion. There is great force in these lines from the "Jovial Cutlers"—

"When does ta mean to get thy *sours* done?
Thy mester wants them in to-day."

Having spent the best part of my life among the working classes, I have not been an indifferent observer of their moral, physical, or intellectual condition; and many of these songs have ever been popular with Sheffield workmen. At "loosings," or "foot ales," some of them have been sung by workmen of the "old school," whose reminiscences of their early days must be heard to be appreciated. Some person better fitted by education and leisure would have discharged the editorial duties more efficiently than myself. The only apology I can offer for any defects of mine is, that the work has been accomplished in moments stolen from my slumbers. The cares of a family would not allow me to devote time which duty required to be devoted to more *profitable* pursuits. Should the work prove either amusing or instructing to any class of the community, the labour bestowed will not be regretted. And, if the book should prove a nucleus round which some more intellectual collector of "Local Songs and Traditions" should gather some other fragments that are yet in existence, an interesting work may be produced, and my endeavours in this direction will not have been in vain.

JOHN WILSON.
Sheffield, July 14, 1862.

MEMOIR OF MATHER (1862)

Little is known of Joseph Mather's parentage or of his early history. If his obituary notice be correct he was born in 1737. As no one can be held responsible either for the time or place of his birth, it was no fault of our author that he was ushered into this world in a locality that enjoyed the odoriferous name of "Cack Alley;" my informant however, says that, "vulgar people called it by a more expressive adjective." This delightful region was a "jennel" which led from Lambert-street to Westbar Green. Its name very probably accurately described its sanitary condition. In early life Joe was apprenticed to the file trade, and he has sung about his profession in the "File Hewer's Lamentation." The general opinion about him is that, in early life, he belonged to the Methodists, and among that people he acquired the knowledge of the Bible which he frequently quotes: in fact it is nearly the only book he refers to in the whole of his songs. Even some of his coarsest pieces end with a moral drawn from the sacred writings. In appearance he was low in stature, but his breadth fully compensated for any deficiency in height. His countenance was remarkable for gravity, and this gave effect to his rebukes. On one occasion, when he was singing "Frank Fearn," a well-dressed bystander rather hypercritically took him to task for using the word "pate," declaring it to be a vulgarism only used by the illiterate. Mather quickly silenced this learned philologer, by declaring that if he would read the 16th verse of the 7th Psalm, he would find these words: "His mischief shall return upon his own head, and his violent dealings shall come down upon his own pate." Some person produced a Bible and verified Mather's words, which utterly discomfited the critic.

It is not unlikely that the artisans as a whole worked less regularly in Mather's days than at present. He was employed by Mr. Nicholas Jackson, of Shemeld-croft; and it was not unusual for the grinders who worked at the Park wheel, to persuade Mather to leave his employment and go to the public-houses frequented by employers of labour, or other persons deemed obnoxious, and in their presence to sing his satirical productions. It therefore often happened that not only *Mondays* were spent as *saint days*, but many other days of the week. If "Bully Idle's Prayer" had then been written, Mather and his companions would have fervently joined in the following:

> Lord send us weeks of Sundays,
> A *saint's* day *every* day;
> Shirts gratis, ditto breeches,
> *No work* and *double* pay.

As it was necessary to take home something on Saturday nights, if Mather's employer refused to "tip up" for "*sours*," our author used to "raise the wind" by vending his songs in the streets, seated on a grinder's donkey,[5] or on the back of Ben Sharp's bull. Should it chance to begin raining, he would ride the animal into the nearest alehouse, and apologise for his rudeness by declaring that he was afraid the rain would rust his hardware. It is said that he sung "Bad Luck to the Crow and the Owl," (song 4), on the market day, in front of the Cutlers' Hall, when the Magistrates were leaving it after discharging their public duties. The poet had been bound over to keep the peace towards Mr. Batty. It is impossible *now* to obtain much information respecting Mather, his original editor only gives one page about him and his works. It is there stated that "His moral character was we believe unimpeachable, his only failing was, being led too easily by cheerful company into some excesses which he naturally abhorred, as it tended greatly to his hurt and the injury of his family. The working mechanics, who well knew his merits, will justly appreciate his talents, as his satirical pieces often forced masters (reluctantly) to comply with poor industrious workmen's just demands. We can with confidence affirm that we never heard that any difficulties however pressing led him to do an unjust action."

The difficulties here mentioned would be pecuniary ones. In all probability his "Petition to Fortune" exemplified his own condition. That he sometimes enjoyed the hospitalities of Godfrey Fox,[6] is unquestionable. I was once informed by an old friend, that he knew

---

[5] Dr. Holland informs me that he has often heard his father speak of the grotesque appearance of Mather on such occasions. He used to be seated (as Robin Hood seated the bishop), with his face to the animal's tail.

[6] The gaoler of the old gaol, Pudding-lane (King-street.)

a lady whose father used to send her when a girl to the old gaol, with a good Sunday dinner for Mather, *because he was a Jacobin*. Some persons allege that he was the author of those lines which used to be sung on the admission of every new "bird" into the gaol:

> Welcome, Welcome, brother debtor,
> Pay your garnish, don't delay;
> Else your coat will be in danger,
> You must either *strip* or *pay*.

According to Howard's description of the place, it was not likely that the moral condition of its inmates would be improved by sojourning there. The prison philanthropist says, (1778) "For common side debtors of both sexes, there are only two rooms, which are also their night rooms." He adds in a note, that the keeper told him, "that then there were near three hundred warrants, and often many more, but the prison is so small, they could not be executed." Persons were confined for sums as low as sixpence, and the fees very often for alehouse scores.

There can be little doubt that the tone of morals was low at that time, and many things now deemed highly culpable would have been considered venial at the close of the last century. Mather was frequently seen among the recruiting parties that were so numerous in Sheffield after the breaking out of the French War. His singing attracted numbers to the *rendezvous*, who under the influence of drink and excitement accepted the recruiting sergeant's shilling to "serve their king and country." Mather was an attendant at the races and fairs in the neighbourhood. The following circumstance is related about him as happening at Chesterfield.

Our author attended the above-named races to dispose of his songs in order to put money in his pocket. Before commencing business, he observed an itinerant quack-doctor vending his nostrums, warranted to *cure all the ills* that flesh is heir to, or else *prevent* them. Not wishing to set up a rival establishment, Mather proposed an amalgamation between poetry and physic, but Æsculapius indignantly spurned the offer, whereupon, Mather mounted a table and struck up one of his peculiar tunes, which attracted all the wondering people who surrounded the disciple of

Galen, so that until the poet had disposed of his whole stock, it was utterly impossible for the man of physic to obtain an audience. When "old Joe" had sold off, he gravely admonished the doctor never to despise an offer of kindness from any person.

The last years of Mather's life were embittered by sickness and poverty, and in the solitude of his home he regretted writing so much of a personal character. His mind often recurred to his early impressions, which he never could efface. He received some assistance from the parish, and was visited in his illness by one of the overseers, (Mr. George Bennet, the "Missionary Traveller,") who would be sure to improve the opportunity his visit afforded. He was also visited by the Rev. Walter Griffith, a minister belonging to the Wesleyans, who had good hopes in Mather's death.

The last lines he wrote exhibit a strong devotional feeling, and as they have never been printed, some persons may feel interested in them. They are the following:

My soul, watch and pray,[7]
Nor cease to obey;
And thou shalt be happy
When summoned away.

Mather resided during the latter period of his life in Pond Hill, and he here quietly resigned his breath. His remains were followed to the grave by many of the working classes of the town, who ever regarded him as their champion. He was buried in St. Paul's churchyard, nearly opposite to the Excise Office. The service was performed by the Rev. A. Mackenzie, whom Mather had keenly satirised, under the name of the "Crow." On his grave (which is in the second row from Norfolk-street,) appears this brief inscription:

In Memory of
JOSEPH MATHER,
Who died June 12th, 1804,
Aged 67 Years.

---

[7] These lines have been preserved by my friend, Mr. Jehoida Rhodes, who obtained them many years ago, from a fellow workman who knew the poet. They supply a link in his history.

INTRODUCTION (1862)

It would be impossible *now* to understand the influence Mather exercised over the minds of his fellow workmen, without some acquaintance with their moral, social, and political condition. His influence, whether well directed or not, was powerful, because in him the artizans recognized a champion of labour. This was the secret of his popularity. His coarse invectives were congenial to the thoughts and feelings of his class. It must be remembered that eighty years ago the "schoolmaster was abroad," and the operatives had not received the benefits of the "National" or the "Lancasterian" system of education. The workman, though unable to scan poetic metre, and ignorant of Iambic or Dactylic verse, could thoroughly comprehend and see beauties in such lines as the following, when aimed at an employer:

> "But he gets well remembered what a rogue he has been,
> In extending dozens from *twelves* to THIRTEENS."

Such expressions would meet with more sympathetic responses than the choicest poetic beauties. If there is one point on which Sheffield workmen are more sensitive than another, it is in upholding the price of labour. Not to do this, is almost an unpardonable offence. It is not unusual for men who make no boast of morals, to declare exultingly that they have always "stuck up for't price."

The writer would never wish this laudable principle to become extinct in the minds of his associates, but he feels assured that the object can be most successfully accomplished by lawful means.

The moral condition of Sheffield during the infancy of Mather will be best understood by the relation of actual occurrences. The *Local Register*, under the date of May 3, 1743, says: "The Wesleyan Chapel in Pinstone-lane demolished by rioters." At the close of the following year occurs this entry: "Mr. E. Bennett's Methodist Chapel in Pinstone-lane attacked and partly destroyed by a mob." These items sufficiently show that freedom of worship was then unknown. The following account of the Rev. Charles Wesley's visits recorded in his Journal relates one of these disturbances: "We returned to our brother Bennett's and gave ourselves to prayer. The rioters followed, and exceeded in outrage all I have seen before. Those of Moorfields, Cardiff, and Walsall, were *lambs* to these. As there is no king in Israel, I mean no magistrate in Sheffield, every man doeth as seemed good in his own eyes." On another occasion, says the author of "Methodism in Sheffield," while John Wesley and the congregation were within, the mob formed the design of pulling down the preaching house. "It was a glorious time with us," says Wesley. "Every word of exhortation sank deep, every prayer was sealed, and many found the spirit of glory resting upon them." The next day the house was completely demolished, not one stone being left upon another. "Nevertheless," says Mr. Wesley, "the foundation of God standeth sure," and "we have a house not made with hands, eternal in the heavens." The next day Wesley again preached in the street, somewhat more quietly than before. In the evening the rioters became more noisy, and threatened to pull down the house in which Mr. Wesley lodged. He went out to them, read the riot act, and gave a suitable exhortation, and they soon afterwards separated, when *peace was again restored*. These were trying times, and required great boldness on the part of Wesley's followers. Mr. Everett, in his "Methodism in Sheffield," says "Through the whole of the winter (1766) Mulberry-street chapel[8] was beset within and without by those disorderly ruffians who were encouraged by their buffoon general. The cloaks and gowns of females were frequently cut with knives and scissors. At other times the chief entered the chapel in harlequin attire, with a cat or a fowl concealed beneath his clothes, which by torturing continued to mew or chuckle, to the great annoyance of both preacher and people; keeping up the laughter of his companions at the same time by every species of buffoonery. When expelled from the interior of the building he contrived to scale the roof, where, in front of a large skylight nearly over the pulpit, he attempted to mimic the preacher. Unable to practise this as often as he wished, and irritated by the repeated checks which he received, he and his associates assailed the windows. Such was the violence employed that the friends were driven to the necessity of having shutters for the windows both above and below, the

---

[8] Messrs. Woodward's paper warehouse. It was the *Independent* Office some years ago.

impressions of the hinges of which are still visible in the window frames of the old buildings. This being done they were still annoyed by the noise of bricks, stones, or other instruments, playing against the wood."

In addition to these riotous propensities, drunkenness, the parent of numerous physical as well as moral evils, was the besetting sin of the times. This baneful practice was not confined to the "lower orders": many of the clergy and the "upper ten thousand" were constantly setting the bad example. In the chapter "on manners," in "The Progress of the Nation," Mr. Porter says "The addiction of the people to intoxicating drinks had reached such a point in 1730 as to occasion continued debates in parliament, and to call for remedies of a very stringent character. It was then the practice of some publicans to entice their customers with a notice painted on a board outside the house to this effect: 'You may here get drunk for a penny, dead drunk for two pence, and have *clean straw for nothing.*' The legislators of that day to check the abuse proposed a duty of 20s. per gallon, and to prohibit the sale of spirituous liquors by retail. This, germ of a 'Maine law' signally failed to stem the baneful practice." "In March, 1738," Mr. Porter says, "A proclamation was issued to enforce the Gin Act, to protect the officers of justice in their efforts to that end, and threatening offenders with punishment. Within two years from its passing 12,000 people had been convicted under the Act, within the bills of mortality, of whom 5,000 bad been sentenced to pay each a penalty of £100, and 300 people had paid £10 each to excuse their being sent to Bridewell house of correction." It will thus be seen that persons who could pay such sums were not the *poor*. The duties of the magistrates would be more onerous then than now in cases of drunkenness. Such cases now are summarily disposed of, thus: "John Smith, charged with being 'drunk and incapable,' fined 5s. and costs."

It was given in evidence before a parliamentary committee in 1743, that the quantity of spirituous liquors made for consumption in England and Wales, was 19,000,000 gallons. This would give an average of $3\frac{1}{8}$ gallons for each individual. A century later there were consumed by 16,000,000 inhabitants 8,160,985 gallons. This shows a diminished consumption of more than five-sixths, coupled with a gradual advance in the moral and physical condition of the people: and in no condition of society has the improvement been greater than amongst the working classes. The author from whose interesting work these extracts are taken, says: "The style of conversation at the convivial parties of *gentlemen* was then such as would not be tolerated in any decent society at present." He further says: "Coarseness of the same kind, though not in the same degree, was exhibited by *educated* females, and that respectable women, the mothers of families, and the wives of respectable tradesmen, were accustomed to amuse their guests by singing songs that no reputable musicseller or bookseller would admit among his wares." The report of a select committee appointed in 1835, to inquire into the state of education in England and W ales, is replete with information of the highest value concerning the increasing decency of the present age. One of the witnesses, speaking of the habits of masters and tradesmen at the time of his apprenticeship, says: "The conduct of such persons was exceedingly gross, as compared with the same class at the present time. Decency was a very different thing to what it is now. Their manners were such as are scarcely to be credited. I remember when a boy of ten years of age, being at a party of twenty, entertained at the house of a respectable tradesman, who kept a good house in the Strand, where songs were sung which now cannot be more generally described from their *nastiness*; such as no meeting of journeymen in London would allow to be sung in the presence of their families... The ballads sung about the streets, and the books openly sold, cannot be adequately described. I have given you in *writing* the words of some common ballads, which you would not think fit to be uttered in this committee. At that time the songs were of the most indecent kind; no one would mention them in any society now; they were publicly sung and sold in the streets and markets." It will be seen from these extracts that Mather's faults were those common to the age in which he lived, and to judge him by our present standard would be evidently unjust. It would be needless to expatiate further on this topic; but it must be remembered that prejudices are stronger, and remain in force much longer, amongst the uneducated than amongst the more highly favoured portion of the community.

The social condition of the operatives of Sheffield was powerfully influenced by several causes, which began to operate about the middle of the 18th century. These causes created a *demand for lab*our, which brought about its effect, viz., a high rate of wages. So early as the year 1720, the operatives of Sheffield combined for trade purposes. The Tailors' Benefit Society (established September 20 that year) was a "short hour movement." The laws against combinations were very tyrannical: as men could not *openly* join together for *trade purposes* they did it covertly as benefit societies. As the Tailors' Society is the *first* "trade union" known to the writer, its constitution may prove interesting. "Whereas, we usually work abroad, at other people's houses, from six o'clock in the morning until eight in the evening, for a day's work, and we now find the same prejudicial to us, and do *all of us* think it too long confinement for one day's work; therefore, it is mutually agreed, &c, that we will not at any time hereafter work abroad for any person or persons whatever, in their houses, longer than six o'clock in the evening, nor begin before six o'clock in the morning, upon any account, occasion, or pretence whatsoever, under the penalty of five shillings of current money of Great Britain for each offence proved on the testimony of two credible witnesses." It would have been interesting if the rate of wages had been given in this document. In the Workhouse accounts for February 7, 1759, occurs the following entry: "Taylor's wages, one week, three shillings." The history of this society would have been very interestingly described by the reverend author of "Alton Locke."

The following extract from the second and third of Edward VI, chap. 15, will show the tyranny of legislation enacted *against* labour: "That if any labourer, artificer, &c. should conspire, covenant, or promise that they should not make nor do their works, but at a certain rate, &c, or should not work but at certain hours and times, they shall forfeit—for the first offence, £10, or else should suffer for the same offence twenty days' imprisonment, and shall only have bread and water for his sustenance: and for the second offence, £20, and in default of payment to *stand in the pillory*: and for the third offence, £40, and in default *to sit in the pillory and lose one of his ears*, and shall at all times after that be taken as a man infamous, and his saying, deposition, or oath, not to be credited in any matter of judgment." It will be seen that the artizans braved the terrors of the law, and combined in defiance of it. Other societies sprang up after the tailors, whose names indicate a trade origin. In 1727, advertisements appeared offering great advantages to filesmiths to settle in France. The *Local Register* says, "Nearly all the workmen began to dispose of their effects, and to pack up their tools for the journey." Upon the recommendation of Judge Jessop, of Broomhall, "a memorial was signed by the principal inhabitants and presented to the king, praying an order in Council to prevent the departure of the workmen." This was followed by a "Proclamation, offering a reward for the discovery of the publishers of the advertisement, and prohibiting the emigration" In 1732 the Filesmiths' Benefit Society was established. This was followed at short intervals by the Cutlers', Old Unanimous, Carpenters', Grinders', Masons', Braziers', and other societies. The principal causes that led to improvements in the *pecuniary* condition of the workmen were, the discovery of silver-plating, the polishing of hardened steel, Huntsman's discovery of making "cast steel," and the establishment of a continental trade.

In reference to this subject, the Rev. Edward Goodwin, in his "Account of Sheffield, 1797," says: "About fifty years ago Mr. Joseph Broadbent first opened an immediate trade with the Continent. In 1751 the river Don was made navigable to within three miles of the town, which greatly facilitated the conveyance of goods abroad. A stage wagon to London was set up by Mr. Joshua Wright. Master manufacturers began to visit the metropolis, as well as other parts of the kingdom, in search of orders, with good success. Several factors now established a correspondence with various parts of the continent, and engaged foreigners as clerks in their counting-houses." The previous state of the town Mr. Goodwin thus describes: "During a considerable part of the present century the Sheffield manufacturers discovered more labour than ingenuity. The workmen durst not exert their abilities for fear of being overstocked with goods; their trade was inconsiderable, confined, and precarious. None presumed to extend their traffic beyond the bounds of this island, and most were content to wait the coming of a casual trader, or to carry their goods with much labour and expense to an uncertain market. It is well known that the chief produce of the manufactory was carried weekly by a few packhorses (Mr. Newsome's) to the metropolis, the inhabitants viewing them passing up the Parkhill with the highest pleasure." This description reminds us of primitive times, and prepares the way for those mechanical improvements before named. The discovery of silver-plating was made about 1743, by an ingenious member of the Cutlers' Company, Mr. Thomas Bolsover. Being engaged in repairing a knife handle made of silver and copper, he conceived the idea of uniting the two so as to form a cheap substance, presenting an exterior of silver. The inventor afterwards established a manufactory for this material. In 1761 Mr. Joseph Hancock made further improvements in manufacturing "Sheffield plate," by producing numerous articles that were formerly made of silver.

The social condition of the workmen in the plated trade is graphically described in "The Autobiography of Samuel Roberts." After describing his early reminiscences, at page 37 he says, "About 1763, Mr. Winter and my father joined Mr. Morton and four others in the manufacture of all kinds of goods, *except candlesticks*, the making of which Mr. W. was to retain to himself. The plated trade had then become considerable, there being about six houses engaged in it, and almost all kinds of goods had then become made of plated metal which had been made of silver. As the trade was completely new in Sheffield, where no similar goods of any metal had been made, workmen at all qualified to make them had to be sought for from London, York, Birmingham, Newcastle, &c. Those who chose to come were, of course, generally indifferent characters, many of them very bad ones; therefore, during the first forty years the journeymen platers were, as a body, the most unsteady, depraved, and idle of all other workmen. They were not only depraved themselves, but a source of depravity in others—in fact, in many respects, a pest to the town. The masters could neither do without them nor obtain better: they were, therefore, forced to give them high wages, and to wink at their irregularities. From this cause the masters were continually enticing the workmen from each other's houses, giving them money to *hire* with them, and letting them get into debt as a kind of security. There were, in consequence, frequent disputes between masters and workmen, and between masters and masters respecting them, so that they almost occupied all the time of the patient Mr. Wilkinson (the vicar), and the *impatien*t Mr. Athorpe, during one day a week in the little old room at the Cutlers'-hall." As Mr. Roberts applies the adjective "impatient" to Mr. Athorpe as a magistrate, it is not unlikely that Mather only sang the popular opinion in calling him "Beef-headed Bob," in the fourth song, or in the invectives displayed in the "Raddlenecked Tup," and the "Norfolk-street Riots." At page 38, Mr. Roberts says: "The masters suffered too much of all kinds of drunkenness and profane swearing[9] in the workshops, and once a year, about September, they gave a kind of saturnalia, called the candle-light supper, at a public-house in the neighbourhood, where the workmen, the work-women, the masters, and the masters of other trades connected with them, were all '*hail fellows, well met.*' " These, however, were the days when silversmiths drank wine with their employers at the King and Miller, and refused to associate with workmen belonging to worse paid trades.

The introduction of polishing steel dates from 1761, when Mr. Robert Hinchliffe "produced the first scissors that were *hard* polished." This discovery would find 25 per cent additional labour for the grinders, and on account of the difficulty of obtaining workmen, more than that amount of additional wages.

Huntsman's invention, in 1770, of cast steel, gave an additional impetus to the staple trades of the town, which is still retained. These causes combined improved the pecuniary condition of the operatives, but too frequently the high wages were spent in demoralizing pursuits.

The *intellectual* condition of the inhabitants must have improved about the middle of the 18th century, because in 1754 was established the first number of that modern educator, the newspaper. This predecessor of our *Independents, Times*, and

---

[9] These practices must have been very common. On the 23rd of July, 1787, was issued "A Proclamation against the profanation of the Lord's day, drunkenness, swearing, and cursing, and other disorderly practices." This proclamation called on the magistracy to be vigilant in enforcing its contents. The following extract from the *Register*, of Oct. 13th, 1787, shows that in Sheffield, at least, the proclamation was not a dead letter: "Last week were committed to prison four persons for swearing, four for drinking and tippling, and five for being drunk."

Telegraphs, was called *Lister's Sheffield Weekly Journal*. Its price was twopence, and moderate-sized advertisements were inserted at 2s. 6d. each. In the following year appeared *The Sheffield Weekly Register*, or *Doncaster Flying Post*. This journal was printed at Doncaster. The literary taste of our ancestors received a further stimulus by the formation of "The Town Library," in 1771. The influence of newspapers and the library would, doubtless, disseminate varied information of the political state of the country. The close of the American war of independence led to renewed agitation for an improvement of Parliamentary representation. So far back as 1733, Mr. Bromley moved the repeal of the Septennial Act. Other attempts were made for "reform" in 1745 and 1758. Dr. Paley remarked in "The British Constitution," that "there was nothing in the British constitution so remarkable as the irregularity of the popular representation. The House of Commons consists of 558 members (the number in 1785), of whom 200 are elected by 7,000 constituents, so that a majority of these 7,000, without any title to superior weight or influence in the state, may, under certain circumstances, decide a question against as many millions." In 1782, 1783, 1785, the question of parliamentary reform was brought before the House of Commons by Mr. Pitt. This subject was congenial to the feeling of the unrepresented throughout the country, and nowhere more so than in Sheffield.

In December, 1791, the "Society for obtaining Constitutional Information" was founded in Sheffield. Political feeling became so rancorous that feuds between neighbours were as common as ever they were between the fiercest theological controversalists. The news of the French Revolution was received in Sheffield with the greatest delight. Paine's "Rights of Man" was proscribed by Government, and as a consequence became more popular than ever. In this situation, on the 8th of May, 1793, Mr. Grey (Earl Grey, of the Reform Bill,) presented a petition to the House of Commons from the "Society of the Friends of the People." It occupied half-an-hour in reading, and stated with propriety and distinctness the defects which existed in the representation of the people. It pointed out and complained of the evils arising from the long duration of Parliaments. The petition stated that a majority of that honourable house were returned by not more than fifteen hundred electors, and that the county of Cornwall sent to Parliament within one as many as the whole of Scotland. It complained of rotten boroughs, of the nomination of members by peers and other persons, and of various other corrupt practices. This memorable debate, in which Pitt, Fox, Sheridan, Erskine, Whitbread, and others took part, terminated by a motion referring the petition to a committee, when 41 voted for and 382 against. Such were the days of rampant toryism. The Government of the day, jealous of every movement of a popular character, enacted laws against freedom of expression, whether with tongue or pen. These things only tended to further exasperate a discontented people, who, unable openly to express their opinions, did so anonymously, through the medium of political squibs. In this class of literature Sheffield excelled.

The feeling in the town at that time may be seen from the notes to songs 26, 27, and 28. The "Poet's Corner" in the *Register* teemed with political satires. The trials of Hardy, Muir, Palmer, and Horn Tooke, were duly chronicled, and the members of the "Constitutional Society" entered into subscriptions to defend printers and authors of works which were not deemed libellous. "Paul Positive" and others wrote for the more educated, while Mather sang in ruder strains to the more illiterate members of society. I have heard a friend, the son of a Jacobin, repeat "The Statesman and his Fool," and exultingly point to its beauties, which he had committed to memory nearly sixty years ago. Pitt's financial policy brought him in for the lion's share of satire. The following are specimens:

"A famous minister of State,
As legendary tales relate,
Oppressed a *foreign* land;
He taxed and tythed, be tythed and taxed:
Greedy as death, he ne'er relaxed
His unrelenting hand.
From every sheep he tore the fleece,
The feathers plucked from living geese,
With his rapacious claws.
He spared not age, nor sex, nor beauty,
Even nose and eyes themselves paid duty,

And *grevious was the tax on jaws*.
In eating, drinking, working, playing,
Sleeping, waking, swearing, praying,
The PEOPLE were for ever *paying*."

In this style was the Government held up to ridicule, and ultimately the "Statesman" was consigned to Hades.

It was such things as these that fixed the stigma of disloyalty on the town. The politicians were divided into "Jacobins" and "Church and king men." The *Register* of April 28, 1793, speaking of the general fast, says: "The churches were *empty*, the taverns *full*. Sheffield is stigmatised as being the seat of ignorance and disloyalty. An opportunity offering to rescue it from at least one part of the imputation, we embrace it by giving the following *liberal* toasts which were drunk by a numerous and respectable company at the 'Bear,' in Norfolk-street. We previously, however, beg indulgence for the authors of them, and hope our readers will not impute these sentiments to a depravity of heart but to some less blameable cause: 'May Tom. Paine live for ever, may he never die, nor nobody kill him, but may he be put in a bag and hung swig swag over hell's gate till doomsday.' 'May the devil sweep hell with the enemies of the king, and afterwards burn his broom.' The proclamation of a fast day called forth the following parody on the "Generals":

"First General Brunswick made a sad campaign,
Then General Coburg took the field in vain,
Next General Wunnser bid the troops advance,
Then General York declared he'd conquered France:
All the vain efforts of *these* Generals past,
We rest our *hopes forlorn* on "GENERAL FAST."

The Farmer's Petition contains some humour at the expense of Mr. Pitt. It says:

"Immortal Pitt, we pray thee to impart
To us thy *slaves* some portion of thine art,
Instruct us from our *oxen* to obtain
The streams which daily from our *cows* we drain.

> Thy head we know is fertile, *ours* are dull,
> Or how a *milch cow* could'st thou make John Bull ?

In contrast to the loyal toasts proposed at the "Bear," stands the conduct of the Jacobins. On the news arriving in Sheffield of the success of the French armies, on November 30th, 1792, the reformers celebrated the event in a remarkable manner. An ox was purchased by subscription, and roasted whole in a field adjoining the town. It was "spitted" about nine o'clock on Monday night, and taken down about two on Tuesday afternoon. It was then divided into quarters and drawn through the streets, amidst the firing of cannon and the acclamations of about six thousand people. Three of the quarters were distributed to the poor in different parts of the town. The remainder was sent to the prisoners confined for debt in the gaol. In the procession was a caricature painting, representing as Britannia, Burke riding on a swine; a figure, the upper part containing the likeness of a Scotch secretary, and the lower that of an ass. The latter was dragging Britannia into a pit. A figure was attempting to stab her with a spear, while the pole of liberty lay broken on the ground. The banner was inscribed "Truth is a libel;" while the sun was seen breaking from a cloud, and the angel of peace was dropping "The Rights of Man" from one hand and extending the other to raise up Britannia. Another flag was inscribed the "Republic of France." Two other silk banners were inscribed "The glorious Congress of Brussels, in which liberty and prosperity were secured. The armies of France have conquered tyrants, and by just laws liberty and reason will conquer the world."

The festivities were upheld during the following week. Some of the more ardent reformers expressed their joy by illuminations. One person exhibited a banner on which was this expressive motto: "The swinish multitude: may they always have the spirit to grunt their disapprobation of evil men and evil manners!" The following year the "Constitutional Society" continued to agitate for parliamentary reform." On April 8th, a public meeting on the Castle-hill (Mr. Gales, chairman,) resolved "That a reform in the representation of the people in Parliament is necessary for the peace and happiness of the country, and that a petition be presented to the house of commons praying for the *thorough reform thereof*." This petition was rejected by the House of Commons for containing disrespectful expressions.

Another open air meeting was held (December 16,) in the Park, of the friends of freedom and parliamentary reform. Resolutions were carried in favour of reform, and condemnatory of Government prosecutions for seditious writings and libels. Sheffield was also duly represented in the "Reform Conference," at Edinburgh, during the year. If *perseverance* could have commanded success, the Sheffield Reformers must have conquered. Another public meeting of the "Friends of Reform" was held in an open piece of ground in West-street, at which it was estimated that 5,000 persons were present. The meeting "declared its abhorrence of the present war carried on against France—the landing of Hessian troops in England without the consent of Parliament," &c.

Similar assemblages throughout the kingdom caused the Government to suppress "seditious meetings," by the strong arm of the law. Many of the reform leaders were arrested, among others the Sheffield delegate (Mr. C. Brown) to the Reform convention. This event took place on the 10th of March. The Reformers, nothing daunted, called another meeting on Castle-hill.[10] That the sentiments expressed by the "Jacobins" were popular, will be observed from the fact that the weekly sale of the *Register* increased from 1468 copies in October, 1793, to 2025 on the first of May, 1794. It was on that day that proposals were published for the establishment of a corps of "Independent Sheffield Volunteers." This body of men, together with the gallant colonel at their head, furnished a frequent theme for the satire of Mather[11] and others. On the 29th of May, William Broomhead (the secretary of the Constitutional Society), William Camage (late secretary), and F. Moody, were apprehended and conveyed to London under a military escort. These arrests were followed up by the apprehension of several inhabitants of the town charged with sedition. Mr. Gales was implicated in these proceedings. It was given in evidence on the trial of Hardy, Horn Tooke, and others, leaders of the popular movement, "that some pikes had been made for the proprietor of the obnoxious Sheffield

---

[10] An account of this meeting will be found in the note to Song 28.

[11] Songs 29 and S3, and notes.

newspaper." The result of this was that Mr. Gales left his country, and the *Register* was, on the 3rd of July, 1794, succeeded by the *Iris*, under the management of James Montgomery and Co. The storm from which Mr. Gales escaped soon burst on the youthful head of his devoted successor (Montgomery), who was convicted on the 22nd of January, 1794, at the Doncaster Sessions, for printing a "patriotic song," written by a clergyman at Belfast. This song was deemed "libellous," although it had been printed two years before. For this offence he was sentenced to three months' imprisonment in York Castle, and fined £20. The libel was the following lines:

Europe's fall on the contest's decision depends;
Most important the issue will be;
For should France be subdued, Europe's liberty ends;
If she triumphs, the world will be free!

If this was *libellous*, well might Paul Positive say:
"And *grievous* was the tax on *jaws*."

It would, no doubt, be gratifying to the imprisoned bard to find that he was not forgotten by the Reformers of the country. At a dinner at the Crown and Anchor, Strand, in honour of the acquittal of Hardy and the other patriots, the following toast was enthusiastically drunk: "Mr. Montgomery—may conscious integrity support him through his present sufferings, and may those sufferings conduct him to a higher period of prosperity and happiness." The prosecutions instituted by Government against persons who only wished for constitutional changes, appear to have been contemptible. A great alteration for the better has taken place in the opinions of both the Government and the people. What could be more ridiculous than the old Tory toasts, "The land we live in, and those who don't like it, them let them leave it." Or the *devout* cry of "The Church and King —your eyes, — every mortal who wishes for liberty."

This severity on the part of the authorities only caused fiercer shafts of ridicule to be hurled at the ministry of the day. "The blessings of Billy's budget, or the heaven born-tinker," was a satire on Pitt. In this pamphlet, which contained a striking likeness of

"Billy," cut in block, the heaven-born tinker has turned preacher and expounds the following texts:

"My transgression is sealed up in a bag," Job chap. 14, v. 17. "He made a pit and digged it, and is fallen into the ditch which he made." Psalm vii. v. 15. "I saw a star fall from heaven unto earth, and unto him was given the key of the bottomless pit." Rev. ix., v. 1. Such productions as these would tell on an oppressed people, because it must be remembered that the year 1795 was one of severe suffering, which greatly intensified the political agitations. That little was needed to render a person suspected, may be seen from this circumstance: "In November, 1795, Francis Ward, of Westminster, a peruke maker, was brought before the magistrates, charged with having *a seditious sign*, viz.— "Citizen Ward, shaver to the swinish multitude." The magistrates told Mr. Ward that he was an impudent man to have such inflammatory language painted on his board. Mr. Ward said that he had a *right* to put anything on his sign-board that pleased him, provided he did not molest any one else. After a long examination the magistrates descended from threats to persuasion, to have the sign taken down, and Mr. Ward was discharged. The board not being removed, the clerk of the magistrates went two days afterwards to Mr. Ward's landlord, requesting him to interfere on account of the seditious sign. Whether it was owing to the landlord's Jacobinical propensities or otherwise, the account does not inform us, but he refused to interfere, declaring that he had no right to dictate to his tenant what he should have painted on his sign. On the Friday following Mr. Ward was apprehended and taken before five magistrates. They expressed surprise that, after the lenient manner in which he had been treated, he should still persist in keeping up the obnoxious board. Mr. Ward alleged that it brought him much custom, and that he had taken counsel's opinion about it. The bench were very desirous of knowing the counsel's opinion on this knotty point of law. This, however, for some time, Mr. Ward declined to tell. After some persuasion the important secret was divulged. The legal opinion was: "that the political barber was a blockhead for putting the sign up; and that the magistrates were bigger blockheads for interfering to pull it down!" The bench dismissed the case, but required the 'knight of the lather brush' to give security for his good behaviour."

The condition of the town may be seen from the following extract from the *Iris*, April 7th, 1797. It is taken from a notice of a "Tour through England and Wales," by Mr. John Houseman. "The manufacturers of Sheffield earn great wages, but are much addicted to drinking: the origin of every other vice. Much distress prevails at this time on account of the high price of provisions, (this must refer to 1795,) and a riot is expected every day. The farmers are consequently afraid of bringing their corn to market, lest it should be taken from them, and only two loads of wheat appeared on the last market day." Though great distress prevails at present the farmers confidently bring their corn to market, and find as good customers and as much honourable dealing as in any town in the kingdom. The social condition of Sheffield is manifested by the fact disclosed by the census of 1861, that in population and rateable value of property it has outstripped nearly every other place; while the number of separate tenements and parliamentary voters bear a greater proportion to the population than any borough in the kingdom. These things speak well for our political condition. At the time of Howard's visit to the Sheffield prisons (1788) he says: "The faulty apprentices are sent to Wakefield House of Correction, where they are often ruined by associating with criminals." It is needless to pursue this subject, because many of the annotations to the songs further elucidate the moral, social, and political condition of the country. It is, however, a cause of great satisfaction to every right-minded person that in these particulars, during the present century, our country has made material progress.

PREFACE TO 1811 VERSION

The author of the following songs not having the advantage of a liberal education, may be justly said to have been self-instructed; bred to a mechanic profession by no means a lucrative one, he of course had but little leisure for reading or study, his reading was chiefly the Bible, which he often quotes. As to his propensity to lash vice and immorality, however dignified the characters; he held it as a just maxim that all who are afraid of having their conduct examined, of what station soever they be, who prohibit all questions concerning their conduct, do by their prohibition confess they are tyrants or impostors, whether kings, priests, magistrates, or masters. Many of the objects of his most satirical pieces are now no more, they are therefore beyond the reach of public censure whatever might have been their failings in life.

His moral character was, we believe unimpeachable, his only failing was being too easily led by cheerful company into some excesses, which he very naturally abhorred, as it tended greatly to his hurt, and the injury of his family. The working mechanics who well knew merits will justly appreciate his talents, as by his satirical pieces, often forced masters (reluctantly) to comply with poor industrious workmen's just demands. We can with confidence affirm that we never heard that any difficulties, however pressing, led him to do an unjust action.

Unlearn'd he knew no Schoolman's subtle art;
No language but the language of the heart.

SONG I
THE FILE HEWER'S [12] LAMENTATION
Tune— "A Pilgrim Blithe and Jolly."

Ordained I was a beggar,
And have no cause to swagger;
It pierces like a dagger—
   To think I'm thus forlorn.
My trade or occupation
Was ground for lamentation,
Which makes me curse my station,
   And wish I'd ne'er been born.

Of slaving I am weary,
From June to January!
To nature it's contrary—
   This, I presume, is fact.
Although, without a stammer,
Our Nell exclaims I clam her,
I wield my six-pound hammer
   'Till I am grown round-back'd.

I'm debtor to a many,
But cannot pay one penny;
Sure I've worse luck than any;
   My traps are marked for sale.
My creditors may sue me,
And curse the day they knew me,
The bailiffs may pursue me.
   And lock me up in jail.

As negroes in Virginia,
In Maryland or Guinea,
Like them I must continue—
   To be both bought and sold.
While negro ships are filling
I ne'er can save one shilling,

---

[12] The term file hewer (cutter) is lost.

And must, which is more killing,
   A pauper die when old.

My troubles never ceased,
While Nell's bairn time increased;
While hundreds I've rehearsed,
   Ten thousand more remain;
My income for me, Nelly,
Bob, Tom, Poll, Bet, and Sally,
Could hardly fill each belly,
   Should we eat salt and grains.

At every week's conclusion
New wants bring fresh confusion,
It is but mere delusion
   To hope for better days,
While knaves with power invested,
Until by death arrested.
Oppress us unmolested
   By their infernal ways.

A hanging day is wanted;[13]
Was it by justice granted,
Poor men distress'd and daunted
   Would then have cause to sing—
To see in active motion
Rich knaves in full proportion,
For their unjust extortion
   And vile offences swing.

SONG II
THE AUTHORS PETITION TO FORTUNE
Tune— from an Air in Midas.

---

[13] Our Criminal laws were cruel at that time. In London alone, during 23 years following 1700, 678 persons were executed for various crimes. Legislators did not see the value of the schoolmaster. No wonder Mather wished to improve the world by strangling the knaves.

Poverty, that vile tormentor,
   Keeps me in strong bonds confined;
Fortune quits me at a venture
   Since I've got a generous mind.
Rags disguise me, friends dispise me,
Bums and lawyers catechise me,
   All against me seem combined.

CHORUS

Wearied bones, despised and daunted,
   Hungry guts and empty purse,
Hung with rags, by bailiff's haunted,
   Prove the times grow worse and worse.

Dunners at my door come knocking,
   And with frowns demand their debts;
Wretched is my fate and shocking,
   Since my wants exceeds my gets.[14]
Thus invested, I'm detested,
Since by poverty arrested,
   Which my brain quite oversets.

Let not care, distress and trouble
   My poor heart so much enslave,
Rather lay the burden double
   Upon some impious knave,
Who for riches nips and twitches—
Though their bags are fill'd like fitches,[15]
   Midas-like, the more would have.

Poverty, that monster frightful,
   Crowds the thoughts with anxious care,
Renders life no ways delightful,

---

[14] "Gets" as a noun has become obsolete though it is very expressive. This word has-escaped the observation of Hunter in his "Glossary of Hallamshire."

[15] "As fall as a fitch" is proverbial—corrupted from *vetches*.

Rather leads to black despair.
Come, be speedy, help the needy;
Of abundance I'm not greedy;
   Give, oh give, me Agur's prayer,[16]

CHORUS

Then calm, peace, and sweet contentment
   Shall subdue my troubled mind,
Turn the point of sharp resentment
   And make friends more mild and kind.

SONG III
MR. BATTY'S MULE

Mr. Batty[17] I've catch'd your mule
   As he was galloping on the highway;
Seeing him run like a resolute fool,
   Caus'd me to think he was going astray.
Some vile neighbour says, Batty, I know,
Gave him bad counsel, which made him do so;
Put him i'th'stable and give him some grains,
And I will recompence thee for thy pains.

Mr. Batty, with grief of soul,
   Says "honest fellow," thou must understand,
This dumb creature, when he was a foal,

---

[16] Proverbs 30, 8.

[17] Mr. John Batty, of Sharrow Head, the mansion now occupied by Wilson Overend, Esq., is the subject of this song. He died December 11, 1789, in his 80th year. The popular opinion is that the "mule" was his son. This is doubtful, unless he died before his father. Mrs Batty died the following year, when the Sharrow Head estates passed by right of marriage to the Rev. Alexander Mackenzie, perpetual curate of St. Paul's, who had married in 1788, Miss Smith, of Sharrow Head, near Sheffield, a niece of Mr. Batty. Many persons will remember "Mackenzie's walk" and will thus see how the name originated. This note will help to explain some allusions in the next song.

Always was subject to my command:
Notwithstanding to him I've been kind,
Now he'll do nothing but what he's a mind;
But if he does not refrain these tricks,
Round-legs shall have him to lead coals and bricks.

Many who bear the Christian name
   Frequently upon their reason intrude;
Then why should we this animal blame,
   Since with *that* he was never endued.
Then let us study sound wisdom to nurse,
Lest like him we grow older and worse;
Through all our proceedings let reason bear rule,
For man is by nature more frail than a mule.

Since in Adam his children fell,
   Each must endeavour to alter the case;
"Cease to do evil, learn to do well,"
   Pray to be changed from nature to grace.
Why should man in his natural state
Boast of his knowledge or think himself great?
Inspir'd wisdom, by faith, has declared
That man to a *wild ass* is compared.

Peradventure he yet may reform,
   When he by poverty shall be brought low,
For want of provender and a long storm
   Soon may cause him himself for to know.
Then his galloping will have an end,
When he has parted with me, his best friend;
Then he'll, like multitudes, when 'tis too late,
Blame his ingratitude—curse his hard fate.

SONG IV
BAD LUCK TO THE CROW AND THE OWL

One day vindicating a mule,

There sprang from the regions below
An infamous, infernal owl,
　In company with a black crow.
The owl being eager of prey,
　Ere I of his claws could get clear,
He robbed me upon the highway,
　For which I was muzzled a year.

CHORUS

Bad luck to the crow[18] and the owl,[19]
　Mat Linen[20] and beef-headed Bob,[21]
That silly old man with his mule.
　And all the infernal black mob.

The crow, his companion and friend,
　Who with him goes prying about;
He was always too idle to fend,
　Which kept him long time in the moult
But since he's deformity wed,
　He swells, and his feathers shine clear;
With dainties he daily gets fed,
　Although I've been muzzled a year.

Each day you may see this vile pimp

---

[18] The Rev. Alexander Mackenzie, M.A., Incumbent of St. Paul's.

[19] Samuel Hall, a vigilant constable, who in company with Mr. M. apprehended Mather for singing "Mr. Batty's Mule." (It was owing to Sam Hall's vigilance in seizing a ballad singer that Montgomery was sent to prison the first time: he was sentenced to three months' imprisonment and fined £20 for printing the song.) The only charge substantiated against our poet was that he had used the name of Mr. Batty: for this he was "muzzled a year," being bound over to keep the peace for twelve months. In his song he castigates all his persecutors under fictitious names.

[20] Matthew Woollen, a constable.

[21] Robert Atthorpe, Esq., a magistrate, and colonel of the Sheffield Volunteers. The epithet, beef-beaded Bob, is very expressive: *vide* his portrait at the Cutlers' Hall.

The dictates of satan pursue,
And surely he's Beelzebub's imp,
   Who has always men's ruin in view.

His infamy, thousands agree,
   Doth penetrate every year;
He thought to assassinate me,
   The day I was muzzled a year.

This black diabolical train,
   The devil but masters them all;
In view an advantage to gain,
   They brought me to Loggerhead's Hall.[22]
With infernal malice and rage
   These ruffins surrounded me there,
And all their black arts did engage,—
   They muzzled me for a whole year.

These pupils, allur'd by Old Nick,
   Against me with more did conspire,—
Because I told knaves of their tricks,
   Like tinder their spirit took fire.
And soon as they did of their base
   Superlative villany hear,
They never could rest in a place,
   Until I was muzzled a year.

My time being fully expired,
   It's proper I vented my mind;
I've done what the law has required,
   So why should my tongue be confined?
'Tis liberty Englishmen claim,
   A privilege counted most dear:
I only embraced the same,
   For which I was muzzled a year.

---

[22] The Old Town Hall at the corner of the church yard.

SONG V
SPENCE BROUGHTON'S LAMENT[23]

Hark, his blood, in strains so piercing,
  Cries for justice night and day;
In these words which I'm rehearsing.
  Now methinks I hear him say—
"Thou, who art my spirit's portion
  In the realms of endless bliss,
When at first thou gav'st me motion
  Knew that I should come to this.

"Though I lie in this condition,
  'Tis not thine appointed will,
Yet it was by thy permission
  That these wretches did me kill.
Thou art free from every evil,
  Witness thine own righteous law:
Cruel men, led by the devil,
  Brought me in the hands of Shaw.[24]

But when time shall be fulfilled,
  How will their guilty conscience roar,
When the youth, whom they have killed,
  Stands before them in his gore!
When the Lord shall come with fury,
  Taking vengeance on his foes,
There no bribed judge or jury
  Will through interest then be chose.

Though you should escape the halter,

---

[23] These lines allude to Spence Broughton, (son of old Broughton, the pugilist,) who was gibbeted on Attercliffe Common, Feb 16, 1792, for robbing the mail, near Carbrook. The night before his execution he sent a very pathetic letter to his wife, which being published in the papers made a strong impression on the public mind

[24] Shaw turned King's evidence, though it is probable that he planned the robbery.

I exhort you to amend.
And for grace your ways to alter
    Importune a sinner's friend.
Though your crimes be more in number
    Than the sands on the sea shore,
Watch and pray, beware of slumber,
    Beg of *Him* to pay the score."

SONG VI
BUGGY EYRE

About eight or nine months ago
    My mind was possess'd with sobriety,
All my acquaintances did know
    I was in a friendly society,[25]
But through a vile plot that was laid,
    Unspeakable loss I sustained;
A cripple I got myself made,
    And many an enemy gained.

CHORUS

'Twas Buggy[26] first led me astray
    By promising me an old hatchet;
I think from his tedious delay
    He never intends me to catch it.

I chanced to be chopping a stick,
    The first day of last January,
When Buggy, employed by Old Nick,
    Came down to our house brisk and airy;
He said if I would with him go,
    A nice little hatchet he'd give me,
But little did I think or know

---

[25] It is probable that Mather was a Methodist at that time.

[26] George (*alias* Buggy) Eyre, one of the constables of the town *vide* Local Register, 1794.

It was his intent to deceive me.

Then quickly I laid down my job,
    And out of the house then he took me,
Forthwith to the head of the town[27]
    And into the Falcon[28] he 'ticed me.
The kitchen was thoroughly lined
    With people both jovial and pleasant;
Amongst them they kept me confined
    Whilst Buggy went out for the present.

Then out of his pint made me drink.
    As free and good-natured as could be,
Yet at the same time I did think
    That was not the place where I should be.
They told mo to ne'er mind the score,
    And hop'd I would not be offended,
Whenever I went to the door
    By two or three I was attended.

When Buggy saw how I was caught,
    For fear I should think him ungrateful,
Instead of a hatchet he brought
    Of roast beef and pickle a plateful.
They tossed the rum bottle about,
    While I in their midst was surrounded,
And ere I could get myself out
    I stay'd till my reason was drownded.
Then some of them ask'd for a song,
    But for a long while I refused;
I had not sung one of so long,
    I begg'd that I might be excused.
Yet harder and harder they press'd,
    Some said for a song they would thank me,
So I took my turn with the rest,
    And thus by their craft they unhank'd me.

---

[27] Barker's Pool was called "top of town."
[28] Cheney-square (New Church-street), so called after Dr. Cheney

SONG VII
NELL AND JOS

Last night, past ten, nigh half an hour,
There coming on a heavy shower,
I stepped aside while it did pour,
   Into a lonesome entry.
There through a broken pane of glass,
Surprised I saw both Nell and Jos,
Who were beyond description cross,
   Throng fighting in the pantry.

Bold Jos was strip'd unto his buff,
With hair untied, exceeding rough,
And Nell, whose nose was daub'd with snuff,
   With her long nails did rake him.
She got both hands into his wool,
Against the door she dash'd his skull,
Although he roar'd like some town bull,
   Most soundly did she shake him.

Then Nell for want of strength and wind
To give it out she was inclined,—
Then Jos began to speak his mind,
   And told her of her gallants.
His hide from wounds had been as free
If drawn through some thick hawthorn tree,
A man worse flogg'd I ne'er did see,—
   Which made him curse her talons,

Before poor Jos put on his shirt
She cast him out amongst the dirt,
His forehead broke, his nose ill hurt,—
   When she her strength regained.
I help'd him up and took him in,
And quickly Nell's warm heart did win;
She dress'd his wounds and wash'd his skin,
   And thus to me complained:

Tomorrow being Sabbath day,
For meat and flour we have to pay,
Tobacco, sugar, soap, and tea,
   And likewise coals and milk, sir.
The half year's rent is just at hand,
And different debts upon demand,
I'm fit upon my head to stand—
   Since no man I can bilk, sir.

This night for us, and three in bed,
He's only brought a poor sheep's head;
One shilling, and three cakes of bread
   Is all in our possession.
Since Jos has took no better care
The wool and horns shall be his share,
Unless he'll eat the bones when bare
   For this his past transgression.

SONG VIII
TIMBER-LEGG'D HARRY

When timber-legg'd Harry crook'd Jenny did marry,
   They were not at all apprehensive of blows;
Three ragmen did quarrel about their apparel,
   Which often had frightened both small birds and crows.
This resolute prial[29] fought on battle royal,
   While Jenny spoke thus, with hump back and sharp shins:
"Be loving as brothers, well chant for some others,
And you shall take ours for some needles and pins."

The bridesmaid, full-breasted, both vowed and protested
   She never saw men at a wedding so rude;
Old Grace with her matches, quite full of her catches,
   Swore she would be tipsy ere they did conclude.
The supper being ended, they each condescended
   With wholesome hot liquor to fill up their skins;

---

[29] Trio

Jack Tar in his jacket, who sat by Doll's placket,
   Swore he would drink nothing but grog and clear gin.

Blind Ralph, with his fiddle, was placed in the middle,
   Who had not been shaved since the second of Jane;
Young Sandy the piper told Moll he would stripe her
   If she would not dance now his pipe was in tune.
They played them such touches that wood legs and crutches,
   And rag-pokes[30] and matches and songs flew about:
Blind Ralph being a stranger, his trap was in danger.
   So he tenderly begged that they would give it out.

Then Ralph was intreated in state to be seated,
   Upon an old cupboard the landlord had got;
Like madmen enchanted they tippled and ranted
   'Till down came the fiddler as if he'd been shot;
They drank gin by noggins, and small beer by flagons,
Till each had sufficiently loosen'd his hide,
   Then all who were able retired to the stable,
And slept with their nose in each others backside.

SONG IX
SHEFFIELD RACES. No. 1

Misers may stay with their treasure,
   Who eagerly mammon embraces;
This is the season of pleasure,
   Come lasses and lads to the races.
Johny to treat his fair
   Has just drawn part of his wages;
Harry and Ruth, this year,
   Are come to renew their ages.

CHORUS

John, with his old grey mare,

---
[30] Rag-bags

As hard as he could pelt her,
Yesterday came to the fair,
  To see them helter-skelter.

Dolly, that crooked old woman,
  Who was sister to full-breasted Mary,
Swore she would go to the common,
  Conducted by splay-footed Harry,
There to meet sharp-shinned Dick,
  And squint-ey'd Poll, with her garters;
Bandy legg'd Ralph and Mick,
Bare four feet five and three-quarters.

CHORUS

Roger came driving Kate,
A pace enough to melt her,
Fearing they should be too late
To see them helter-skelter.

See, now they go off with a clatter,
  The horse that can win it shall wear it,
Jockeys well versed in the matter
  Exert their whole power to clear it;
With shouts that rend the sky
  And put to a consternation
Numbers of birds that fly
  And part of the brute creation.

SONG X
SHEFFIELD RACES. No. 2

Come, ye lads and lasses gay,
  Lay aside your toil and labour,
Joy and mirth begin to-day,
  Call upon each friend and neighbour;
All as one united be

To partake of things diverting,
At the races you will see
Man and horse their powers exerting.

CHORUS

Bacchus, O thou god of wine,
This week holds us to exalt thee;
Bastards only will repine.
Free-born sons disdain to fault thee.

Hark, the bells begin to ring
   To invite all loyal people,
Enemies to church and king[31]
   Wish they may shake down the steeple.
Such to him may lie and prate.
Cant and censure man and woman,
We'll go see who wins the plate,
Come let's haste towards the common.[32]

Now the colours are displayed,
   And the music plays most charming,
Let no mortal be dismayed,
   Nothing interferes, alarming.
View aloft the shining purse,
   With such pomp and splendour guarded,
With the same the winning horse
   For his toil shall be rewarded.

See, they're off, away they scour,

---

[31] This was written many years before Burns wrote—
   "Wha will not sing God bless the King
      Shall hang as high the steeple;
   But while we sing God bless the King,
      Well not forget the people."

[32] The races on Crookesmoor or common were discontinued in 1782. The commons were not enclosed until 1791, when serious riots occurred in consequence.

Whip and spur are both in action,
Man and horse exert their power
   To yield sportsmen satisfaction.
Elevated by huzzas.
   See, they push and change their places;
Such diversion for three days
   We expect at Sheffield races.

Thursday's race is for a cup,
   Neatly chased and ornamented,
Helter-skelter cutting up
   There will be, 'tis represented.
And when Friday's plate is won
   Let us lay these lines before us,
Friendly talk of what's been done,
   Drink about and join this chorus.

CHORUS

Thank thee, Bacchus, god of wine,
   For thy aid in past enjoyment;
Now, be it each one's design
   To retire to his employment.

SONG XI
JEZEBEL'S DAUGHTER
Part I

Last Friday, at dinner time, who should I see,
But Jezebel's daughter come riding so free:
As soon as she did nearer approach
I found she had got into Watson's stage coach.[33]
Thought I to myself, thou seem'st for to swell,
A sow would become a king's palace as well.

---

[33] James Watson, the first landlord of the Tontine Inn, 1789. The fare to Doncaster by Watson's coach was 6/6: *vide* Sheffield Register, 1787.

We don't need to wonder the world is at strife,
Since beggars can imitate folks of high life.

I wonder, says one, who they've got in the stage,
That looks so much like an old woman in rage:
Her fine spotted habit, I think for my share,
Would look full as decent upon a cart mare.
She also was dress'd in a cap trim'd with wire,
A sponge in her topping[34] to raise it the higher.
Some of the militia men wickedly swore
She was a great masculine coarse-featured whore.

Besides, she had got a conspicuous head:
No horse-flesh, I'm certain, that's been a month dead
In scorching hot weather stinks worse than her breath;
She ought to be weather-cock'd deep in the earth.
At Leeds she was taken for old mother Bunch,
By some for the wife of my friend Mr. Punch.
Some thought she belonged to a mountebank fool,
While other some thought she was John Addy's doll.

When she had fill'd the whole town with surprise
By telling great numbers of audacious lies,
Her clothes which she borrow'd or bought upon strap[35]
She bundled them up and put under her lap.
A little short pipe in her *mus* she did screw,
As though she belonged to some pedlar or Jew.
Then came slobbing home in a large pair of shoes—
Stout Wharton's the person that brought me the news.

She lobs up and down in a white petticoat,
She bares it nine inches in order to show't.
She told many strangers she bought it when new,
But it sprung from the "pop shop"[36] I know to be true;

---

[34] Topping is nearly obsolete. The hair was worn combed up and high peaked hats fastened on the head by a long pin thrust through them.
[35] On credit; the etymology of the word is very doubtful
[36] 2016 note: pawn shop

Yet, here's the misfortune, it not being wide,[37]
She hasn't got liberty for a great stride.
The reason,—it bound her so fast o'er the rump,
When crossing the sink she was forced to jump.

Astride of a water pot, often half drunk,
Two lusty men's shoes and her stockings much sunk,
A pair of scabbed hands and her head dress'd in taste,
To be big with child, she appear'd in the waist.
Her haft-pipe she rested upon a large wem,
A pipe black as charcoal, two inches the stem,
Confined in her mus-hole; prepared to suck biles,
'Twas Jezebel's daughter I saw chopping files.[38]

SONG XII
JEZEBEL'S DAUGHTER
Part II

One day, at my labour, I o'erheard a neighbour,
  Most briefly relating her journey to Leeds,
'Twas Jezebel's daughter, whose mother had taught her
  The art of seduction and many bad deeds.

I gave due attention to all she did mention;
  Well pleased with her story I got it by rote.
The words are verbatim, as she did relate 'em,
Composed to the tune called "shuffle and cut,"
  And these were the words of this snivelling slut:

With a short pipe in my mouth,
  And a pair of men's shoes, about half an ell
I turned my face to the South,
  And returned home to old Jezebel.

---

[37] Our Sheffield lasses now reverse this with crinoline.

[38] Several attempts have been made to prevent women cutting files; the custom, it appears, is old.

When I arrived at my cot,
 The old gipsy was tenting it,
I found it was the same spot,
 But not as I had been representing it.

Slut-holes above and below,
 Spider-webs no one could nominate,
Cat's muck and dog's muck also,
 Shit pots mould and abominate.
Black-clocks, crickets, and mice,
 Rats very daring and impudent,
Millions of bugs, fleas, and lice
 Were wandering over my tenement.

Fretting, alas! was in vain,
 So I composed myself speedily,
Fell to my calling again,
 Baking and thieving most greedily.
Every peck I did bake,
 I nibbled harder than e'er I did;
Yes, I took more by a cake,
 This I am certain and clear I did.

Then did old Jezebel say,
 For thy expenses extraordinary,
Well make the leaven tub pay
 Sixpence a peck more than ordinary.
Yesterday twelve pecks of meal
 Came to be baked in reality,
Twenty-four cakes I did steal,
 Which shows a great deal of frugality.

Twelve pence my wage was at least,
 Had not I cause to look pleasantly,
I got as drunk as a beast,
 How it was I'll tell you presently.
We've a stone bottle in cog,
 A bottle for secresy suitable,

We get it filled up at the Dog.[39]
When we've a mind, indisputable.

If we go seek for some ale,
   A pint or pennyworth with sanctity,
While we are telling our tale,
   The girl fills us treble the quantity,
Corks up the bottle secure,
   Lest they discover our knavery,
Gives it us very demure—
   Thus we do live above slavery.

Tipsy, we then fall asleep;
   When we awake we are dry again:
Close to the bottle we creep,
   Drink deep and then set it down again.
Here's good health to John Shay,
   Who still keeps the bottle replenishing;
He may work hard day by day
   To pay for his liquor diminishing.

We must confess it's not right
   For mortals whose lives are in jeopardy,
Daily to live by the bite,
   And swell us with other men's property.
We deceive women and men,
   All sorts of wickedness cherisheth,
What will become of us when
   The hope of the hypocrite perisheth.

SONG XIII
JOHN OLDHAM'S DISASTER

[40]When all nature was hush'd, bird and beast gone to rest,
   And each temperate man in his bed,

---

[39] The Dog Inn, Spring Street, kept by John Shaw, an industrious gardener, commonly called John Shay.

My heart in an instant with fears was distress'd,
  Peace and sleep to a distance were fled.
This moment each thing was as still as a mouse,
  But the next, to my shocking surprise,
Something quite uncommon did shake the whole house,
  In my life I never heard such a noise.

The bed where I lay jump'd a foot from the place,
  Which made my wife and children quake,
A cratch fill'd with bottles fell down the staircase,
  And they clashed while the kitchen did shake.
Plates, irons, and glasses made different sounds,
  While the clothes on the winterhedge[41] blazed,
At this midnight concert my fright had no bounds,
  So I ran out of doors almost crazed.

It was my intent to have holloed out fire,
  But two neighbours I chanc'd for to meet,
And what was the reason I began to inquire,
  Of the terrible shock in the street.
One said 'tis John Oldham,[42] who's got such a fall,
  'Tis a mercy we are not destroy'd;
Our brewing tubs and gantries are overturn'd all,
  And each one in the house terrifi'd.

Alas! said another, it is not to tell
  What a loss by this shock was sustain'd,
Our sow has got kill'd, by the hog-stye that fell,
  And eleven fine pigs but just weaned.
In short, we concluded our dwelling to quit,
  Which apparently soon must fall down,
Or petition the parliament not to permit
  Such a monster to live in the town.

---

[40] The serious introduction of this song does not prepare anyone for the result.

[41] 2016 note: A clothes' horse

[42] John Oldham, victualler, Fargate, is the person alluded to in this song. John was fat enough for an alderman.

SONG XIV
BEN EYRE[43]

On Sunday morning last,
  We played a trick not fair,
We stole near twenty walking sticks,
  Belonging to Ben Eyre.

Blencorn and him did thwart,
  While we took thick and small,
Then one by one we took them down,
  'Till we had got them all.

To Gosports then we went,
  Where we got ready sale;
To such like drunkards as ourselves,
  We sold them by retail.

When Ben awoke from sleep,
  Thinking to view his store,
From off the balk he miss'd his sticks,
  Lord how he curs'd and swore!

---

[43] The office of constable appears to have been hereditary in the family of the Eyres. Ben was an assistant of his brother Joseph, who was also constable of the markets, and of whom the following incident is recorded. Soon after the opening of the New Shambles in 1788, some of the young men in the service of Messrs. Newton and Porter, grocers, &c, attached a rope to the market bell. After locking up the gates and returning to his home in Shude hill, Eyre was astonished at hearing a violent ringing of the bell, and at once concluding that the thieves had gained access to the market, set out with his favourite dog, "Turk" to apprehend the rascals. To make doubly sure he unlocked one gate and sent "Turk" in to drive them out. With what success, the reader may imagine. This adventure gave rise to a song which seems lost but of which the following is the first stanza:
> "Hey ! Turk, go catch that lurk,
> For thou art very cunning;
> And I'll stand at the gate and crack his pate,
> As soon as he comes running."
> (2017 note: see "Songs not in the 1862 edition")

Then he began to think
  Who had been in his room,
Two blackguard dogs Blencorn and Ben,
  Sure death shall be their doom.

How vex'd was I to think,
  My trouble thrown away;
I went to Wharncliffe for those sticks,
  Upon last New-Year's day.

But since my passion's cool'd,
  I'm will'd to set them free,
I freely do forgive the world,
  And hope the world will me.

SONG XV
FRANK FEARNE[44]

Mortals all in town or city,
  Pay attention to this truth;
Let your bowels yearn with pity,
  Towards a poor deluded youth.

Tho' with Satan's vile injunctions,
  I was forced to comply,
Now it causes sad reflections,
  Since I am condemned to die.

Andrews, O that name! it pierces,
  Thro' my very inmost soul:
And my torments much increases.
  In this glomy condemn'd hole.

At Kirk edge I shot and stab'd him,

---

[44] Fearne was executed at York assizes and afterwards gibbeted on Loxleyedge, March 27th, 1782, for the murder of Nathan Andrews, a respectable watch, maker of High street, Sheffield

  Cut his throat and bruis'd his pate,
Of his watch and money robb'd him,
  Causes my unhappy fate'

Christians pray that true repentance
  May be given a wretch like me.
I acknowledge my just sentence,
  Ther's no law can set me free.

Let me make one observation,
  Though to sin I've been enslav'd,
Through my Saviour's mediation,
  My poor soul may yet be sav'd.

Hark ! I'm call'd to execution,
  And must bid the world adieu !
'Tis the hour of dissolution,
  And my moments are but few.

Let me endless bliss inherit,
  Wash me from my guilty stains:
O, receive my precious spirit,
  Though my body hang in chains.

SONG XVI
LOXLEY EDGE

Last Easter Sunday with bat-stick and trip,
To Pitsmoor[45] firs I did eagerly trip,
  But soon got fast in a quick-set edge;
A Methodist preacher, good natur'd and stout,
Took hold of my shoulders and lifted me out,
And said, "Young man. take advice from a stranger,
Permit me with freedom to tell thee thy danger,

---

[45] Pitsmoor firs, the name yet retained in "Firs Hill," was the Sunday resort of numbers who preferred games at foot-ball and knurr and spell to attending the church.

Thou art in the road to Loxley edge."[46]

I found a desire on that point to be clear,
So I asked him how he could make it appear,
   Since I had my face toward Washford bridge.[47]
Says he I have visited many a cell,
And heard malefactors repeatedly tell,
That breaking the Sabbath doth often contribute,
To lead to the gallows, from thence to the gibbet,
   So thou'rt in the road to Loxley edge.

Whilst thou art transgressing the laws of the Lord,
By murdering the time set apart for His word,
   Thou may'st be assur'd thy soul is in pledge;
Thy heart will grow harder and harder each day,
Thy light become darkness, and thou wilt give way
To Satan's temptations and subtle seductions,
Until thou art ripe for the pit of destruction,
   So thou'rt in the way to Loxley edge.

If thou wouldst be happy my counsel pray take,
And frequent the means that's appointed for grace,
   That I may nothing against thee allege;
Beseech the Almighty to plough up thy heart,
To take away sin and his spirit impart.
Had Fearne ta'en this method, his life had not ended,

---

[46] The incident recorded in this song really happened. Mr. Percival was the Methodist preacher, (they were not "Reverends" then) who so faithfully rebuked Sabbath breaking. The line "beseech the Almighty to plough up thy heart," is characteristic of the early followers of Wesley.

    This song must have been composed while the execution of Fearne was fresh in remembrance. The moral condition of the town may be inferred from the following extract from the Sheffield Local Register, Feb. 12th, 1790: "Nine men put in the stocks for tipling in a Public-house during Divine service, and two boys made to do penance in the Church for playing at trip during Divine service, by standing in the midst of the church with their tripsticks erect."

[47] Attercliffe bridge, called after the Old ford, "Wash-ford."

At Tyburn, near York, nor in chains been suspended,
　Betwixt heaven and earth upon Loxley edge.

SONG XVII
STEVENS & LASTLEY'S EXECUTION[48]

O Wharton, thou villain, most base,
　Thy name must eternally rot;
Poor Stevens and Lastley's sad case
　For ever thy conscience will blot.
Those victims, thou wickedly sold,
　And into eternity hurl'd,
For lucre of soul sinking gold,
　To set thee on foot in the world.

Thy house is a desolate place,

---

[48] This song originated from the following circumstances. On the 30th of Nov. 1789, John Wharton was robbed of a basket of provisions on Lady's bridge. Two men, John Stevens and Thos. Lastley, were executed at York in the following April for the offence as one of highway robbery. In reference to this extract the following from the Sheffield Register of April: "The behaviour of these unhappy men, since their condemnation, manifested a hearty contrition for their crimes and a becoming resignation to their ignominious fate… Much disturbance has arisen in this town since the execution of Stevens and Lastley from an idea that the prosecutor swore to aggravated circumstances which really did not happen. This suspicion has gathered strength from the solemn asseverations of the two unfortunate men communicated in a letter to their shopmates, dated the evening previous to their execution. The populace have several times beset Wharton's house, and hung the figure of a man on a gibbet before his door, but yesterday they were so violent as to break every window and otherwise so much damage the house as to render it scarcely habitable. The current report when our paper went to press, was that Wharton had escaped in woman's clothes."

　　Six men were executed at these assizes, amongst whom was another from Sheffield, named Moore; Booth, named in the song, was transported. I have been informed by an old man that the robbery was intended as a joke, Wharton actually partaking of the roast leg of mutton which was taken from him.

Reduc'd to a shell by the crowd,
Destruction pursues thee apace,
  While innocent blood cries aloud.
Poor Booth in strong fetters thou'st left
  Appointed for Botany Bay,
He is of all comforts bereft,
  To die by a hair's breadth each day.

Depend on't thou never can'st thrive,
  Thy sin will e'er long find thee out,
If not whilst thy body's alive,
  It will after death, without doubt.
When Stevens and Lastley appears,
  Requiring their blood at thy hands,
Tormenting a million of years,
  Can't satisfy justice's demands.

Some others were equally vile,
  To prompt thee to this wicked work;
In order to share of the spoil,
  Thou got by the blood spilt at York.
All are equally guilty with thee,
  And as a reward for their pains,
They ought to be hung on a tree,
  And then be suspended in chains.

SONG XVIII
THE DERBYSHIRE FARMER[49]

A farmer in Derbyshire had a wild son,
That would go a courting let what would be done;
Away he set out without any regard,
What honest man's daughter he injured or marr'd.
His friends and relations were fill'd with disgust,
When he threw the reigns on the neck of his lust;

---

[49] This song relates to a marriage settlement that occurred in a highly respectable family.

Each one was offended, though ever so meek,
For many miles round the D—l's house in the Peak.

Just like some wild jackass, o'er the mountains he stray'd
In search of a female he gallop'd and bray'd.
A length a young damsel he utterly spoiled,
For by his seduction he got her with child.
Her father then promised how liberal he'd be,
If they two to marry would jointly agree:
The knot being tied, the farmer in full,
Produced the girl's fortune—a lousy young bull.

The calf was removed to his father's own farm,
Where there was no want of good hay in a storm;
If ever he bellowed, old Bagshaw would say,
"Hark, yon's thy wife's fortune, go drive him away."
One day he went out in a wonderful air,
And with his ash-plant drove the brute to Hope fair:
The cause of offence to remove as I'm told,
And there he converted his bull into gold.

This done he returns to his parents in peace,
In hope animosities ever might cease.
I cannot but pity his singular case,
His father still throws the bull-calf in his face.
If ever he puts the old man in a pet,
No matter what company there may be met,
He blacks him and calls him a shackle-brain'd elf,
And right in his teeth throws the lousy bull-calf.

CHORUS

So take my advice, ye young men of Foolow,
Of Castleton, Bradwell, and Small-Dale, also;
You'd better live single, than marry by half,
For Bagshaw's wife's fortune—a lousy bull-calf.

SONG XIX
THE CASTIGATION[50]

My song is true, so let it pass,
A horse transform'd into an ass,
Not worthy of the meanest grass,
   Produced by lanes or commons.
With Putty prim'd the other day,
He cock'd his tail, began to bray,
To th' Justice Clerk did trot away,
   And there procur'd a summons.

The paper purchas'd for abuse,
He may apply to dirty use;
The brute is left without excuse,
   Though destitute of reason.
Presumptious beast, insulting clown,
How durst thou look towards my crown,
Much less attempt to pull it down,
   I'd have thee tried for treason.

Though thou display'st thy knavish tricks,
First bites, then turns thy heels and kicks,
E're long, I'll make thee carry bricks,
   And to the coal yard send thee.
Thou animal, despised by hogs,
To thy round legs I'll chain two clogs,
And bait thee oft with butcher's dogs,
   To see if that will mend thee.

The Hawke that soars about thy house,

---

[50] This song is a satire on Round Legs, a carter who lived in Smithfield. He kept five or six asses which were more famed for bone than flesh. Mr. Batty threatens to send his Mule to "Round Legs" as a punishment. See Song III. Mather appears to have equalled Cobbett in nick-naming people, and most bitterly does he satirize Round Legs in another song not included in his previously published collection, but which is given in this edition — the song commencing "Round Legs to Wadsley went."

As poor as any pauper's louse,
For greedy of a little mouse,
   Did villany exhibit;
That knave that's lost a tooth before,
That bird and ass that paid the score,
Bug, prick-ear'd Sam, and many more,
   Deserve to grace the gibbet.

SONG XX
FISH AND TOMMY TICKTACK[51]

An alderman for Satan's use,
   In Tophet slipt the cable,
In order Garbut to reduce,
   But he will not be able.
Though Sambourne,[52] Wilkinson,[53] and Shaw,
   That base militia sergeant,
Ticktack and Bedford joins the cause,
And Fish, the devil's agent.

CHORUS

Then butcher's boys
Let's all arise.
And drive that ruffin quick back.
And all that join
That black design.

---

[51] This song records a riot that took place in the market. Garbut was a "Cheap John," and from the text seems to have been very popular. Oar author extols him, but is very severe on his opponents. It is doubtful who Fish was. The person referred to under the sobriquet of "Tommy Ticktack "was Mr. Thos. Pennington, a respectable tradesman in High-street, who took an active part in public matters. The popularity of Garbut probably arose from his singularity. It appears from a line in the fourth verse that he was clothed in "a hairy dress;" this alone would make him well known.

[52] Mr. Sambourne, deputy clerk of the peace, 1790.

[53] The Rev. James Wilkinson, vicar of Sheffield.

With Fish and Tommy Ticktack.

See Garbut, like a busy bee.
   Improve each shining moment,
And seeks his bread from sea to sea,
   Which well deserves a comment.
Whilst idle drones stay in the hive,
   Extort from friend and stranger,
Conspire against him and contrive
   Because their craft's in danger.

Behold that black insulting crew,
   Who wish to pass for gentry,
Has purchas'd waster goods, in view
   To take in all the country.
Such trumpery was never bought,
   They scarce will hing together,
For which these rascals should be caught,
   And flogged like Fish's father.

This combin'd herd on market days,
   When Garbut mounts the rostrum,
With grudging hearts upon him gaze,
   And sigh for want of custom;
They curse him in his hairy dress,
   Although a man deserving,
His efforts meet with great success,
   Whilst sneaking dogs are starving.

Hooker in opposition stands,
   With Gay in borrow'd habit,
Worse ne'er escap'd the hangman's hands,
   Nor scarce disgrac'd a gibbet.
Those blacks are held in utmost scorn,
   'Midst thousands of beholders,
Whilst Garbut through the streets is borne
   In triumph on men's shoulders.

May that infernal dog of hell,
   Now absent from his region,
Soon re-possess his native cell.
   And take with him a legion;
Such as conspire to starve the poor,
   Of every rank and station,
Likewise each rogue and private whore
   That formed this combination.

Then butchers' boys, &c.

SONG XXI
DR. KELLY[54]

A vile and most abandon'd wretch,
   No friend to man nor nations,
Did kindle with a hellish match -
   Venereous conflagrations;

America soon catched the flame,
   The whore in every alley
Exclaimed against the blasted name
   Of squinting wry-nos'd Kelly.

CHORUS

With gums and tongue as sore as biles,
   And jaws tied up with flannel.
The hunters curse the match and wiles
   Of black infernal Daniel.

Full thirty years he's ranged the globe,
   With blue stone, pills and unction;
And scandaliz'd a genteel robe

---

[54] This song relates to an itinerant quack doctor who had been in the army, and is sufficiently descriptive of the doctors peculiar practice. Mather claimed the right to flagellate quacks of all classes.

With his infernal function.
"Pox-master general" resounds
  O'er ev'ry hill and valley,
The infamy hath got no bounds,
  Of squinting wry-nos'd Kelly.

At Gib' he set the rock on fire,—
  Should any person doubt it,
Among the train he may enquire,
  They'll tell him all about it.
His wife a stinking victim died—
  May Hymen weep for Nelly—
And wished she never had been tied
  To squinting wry-nos'd Kelly.

The god of marriage was unwise—
  Appealed to Cupid's mother:
Tho' one wife fell a sacrifice,
  He soon gave him another.
Now she is fir'd as bad as Nell,
  (The bosom friend and ally,)
By that destructive dog of hell,
  Old squinting wry-nos'd Kelly.

Bold Samson turned his foxes out,
  With firebrands at their arses,
To burn the standing corn, about
  Three hundred took their courses;
Just so the devil slip'd his fox,
  With firebrand at his belly,
That all the world might get the pox,
  Thro' squinting wry-nos'd Kelly.

His villany on foreign shores
  Hath often been detected;
Of stealing bacon, deals, and stores,
  The rascal stands convicted.
His hellish deeds excite disgust,

The universe can tell ye,
The devil I would sooner trust,
    Than squinting wry-nos'd Kelly

SONG XXII
THE HEN-PECKED HUSBAND[55]

Poor John being drinking one day with a friend,
He had but two shillings, and that he would spend,
Which made him uneasy for fear of his wife,
"Nay, truly," says he "I'm afraid of my life."

CHORUS

Try again, Johnny, lad,
Fight like a tiger, lad,
Try again, Johnny lad, conquer or die.

His friend being angry to hear him say so,
To take up his cudgels fool-hot he did go,
The house being dark made the madam to think
It was her poor Johnny disguised in drink.

She seized the poker, his head she did feel,
Altho' a stout fellow she made him to reel;
He returned the blow with a shocking surprise,
For he flatten'd her nose and he swelled up her eyes.

He follow'd his blows till she cried "Spare my life!
Remember, dear Johnny, that I am thy wife;
I own for insulting thee I was to blame,
The fault's in myself, I confess to my shame."

So when that he found her begin to relent,

---

[55] The domestic felicity of poor Johnny and his wife is graphically described in this song. The line: "Who spluttered great words with his heart in his shoes" shows very forcibly that Ruth was John's *better* half.

He went out and left her a while to repent,
Then brought in her Johnny inform'd of the news,
Who spluttered great words with his heart in his shoes.

He call'd for his supper, she brought it in haste,
For fear of his cruelty more she should taste,
Then they went to bed, but poor John could not sleep,
For hearing his wife in such sorrow to weep.

Poor John could not sleep for hearing her sighs,
Much more when he saw her swell'd cheeks and black eyes
O then honest Johnny replied "My dear Ruth,
If thou wilt forgive me I'll tell thee the truth.

A friend unto whom I related my case
Came here in my absence and used thee so base,
For which I am sorry and grieved to the heart,
And wish that I could but partake of thy smart."

These words he had scarcely let go from his lips,
But hold of the bed-stock she eagerly grips,
And with it she did the poor simpleton beat,
Like some able husbandman thrashing of wheat.

He roar'd out for mercy, but all was in vain;
When weary she rested, then at him again;
All manner of colours she painted his hide—
This merciless bedstock was well occupied.

So under the basket poor Johnny remains;
Of her cruel treatment he daily complains:
"I'm under the basket," repeated he cries,
"But might have ruled master if I had been wise."

SONG XXIII
THE CROOKES ROGUE[56]

My name's Blackguard, I dwell at Crookes,
Infernal tempers, sulky looks,
Actions none can justify;
Which makes my neighbours jointly cry,
That's the jockey that bought the goose,
Stole another when it got loose.

Two wings procured, a knave allured
  To swear it was his own when try'd;
Here lies the sequel, they were not equal,
  For both of them chanc'd to belong one side.

  This accusation was too true,
  The goose I bought to Walkley flew;
  I stole a friend's for recompence,
  For which a lawsuit did commence.
  To arbitrators it was put,
    Quite out of feather my goose was out,
These two odd wings so mix'd my springs,
I lost the trial with costs of suit;
The money I tender'd, and thus got render'd
An infamous villain of no repute.

SONG XXIV
NELL AND THE JOURNEYMAN HATTER

Rodney has gotten the day,[57]

---

[56] Somehow or other this portion of Hallam has obtained notoriety for roguery. To "Hallam it" is still proverbial for cheating. Any one acquainted with the spring-knife trade will see much point in the line: "These two odd wings so mix'd my springs."

[57] On April 22, 1782, Admiral Rodney obtained a glorious victory over the French fleet, under the command of the Count de Grasse. In the following month, the gallant Admiral and his crew received the thanks of both

De Grassey is justly rewarded,
The truth I may venture to say
  By some it is little regarded.
The people have chiefly engaged
  To talk of a different matter.
The women are greatly enraged
  At Nell and the Journeyman Hatter.
      Fal, lal, &c

Like a he-goat or jack-ass,
  That ranges the forest all over,
Which cannot a fellow brute pass,
  But what he's inclined for to cover,
Regardless of every one,
  Who ridicule, scoff, and bespatter,
When men to their labour are gone,
  To Nell goes the Journeyman Hatter.

Happy in each other's arms,
  Mistrusting no manner of evil,
One day they were rous'd by alarms,
  Proceeding they thought from the devil,
The soot in such quantities fell,
  Soon ended their amorous chatter.
From sweeps it was hard for to tell
  Miss Nell and the Journeyman Hatter.

One with a long holly hush
  Ascended the house like a martin,
Who sent soot down with a brush,
  Which set them a sneezing and farting;
The one in his breeches let fly,
  The other her urine did scatter,
Which quite put a stop to the joy
  Of Nell and the Journeyman Hatter.

Nell and her sister also,
  Once quilting up-stairs for employment,

Houses of Parliament for their brave conduct.

When hearing her gallant below,
   Nell knock'd for a little enjoyment.
This jockey, without any dread,
   Ascended the stairs with a clatter,
And soon they were upon the bed,
   Both Nell and the Journeyman Hatter.

This is no stranger than true,
   The sister inclined to their notion,
Eight upon the Hatter's back flew,
   Desirous to join them in motion;
So then there was ill upon worse,
   Like frog upon toad back they at her,
Which must be vexation of course,
   To Nell and the Journeyman Hatter.

What shall we do in this case,
   But make a purse by contribution,
Erect a Cuck-Stool[58] at that place,
   To wash them from this pollution.
As Nelly resides at a house,
   Nigh where there is plenty of water,
Come let us assemble and douse
   Both Nell and the Journeyman Hatter.

SONG XXV
HALLAMSHIRE HAMAN[59]

---

[58] This song is more descriptive than delicate. In the last verse the author recommends the "Cuck-stool" as a punishment for their misconduct.

   The "Cuck-stool" (or more properly "Cuckolds,") was a seat erected over a pond or stream on which the culprit was securely seated. The punishment consisted in "ducking" or "doucing" those who were unfaithful to their nuptial vows. This mode of reclaiming offenders has now sunk into oblivion, like the stocks and the pillory.

[59] The hero of this song was Mr. George Wood, scissors manufacturer, of Pea-croft. The second line in the last stanza pointedly alludes to him. At the time the song was written, he was senior warden of the Cutlers'

When Ahasnerus[60] o'er Persia did reign,
Vile Haman by plots did much treasure obtain,
By fradulent stratagems rose to be great,
And caused himself to sit at the King's gate.
The offspring of Belial raised so high,
Great homage demanded of all who pass'd by;
But Mordecai, one of the seed of the Jews,
To honour proud Haman did ever refuse.

Company, and in due time became "Hallamshire's King." There can be little doubt that Mather sung the popular feeling, he being the champion of the Sheffield artizans. The history of this song will not be uninteresting as a contrast to the state of feeling existing between the employer and employed at the present time. In the beginning of 1790 the workmen in various trades asked their employers for an advance of wages. This not being conceded a strike for the advance took place in August. On the 27th of that month, the "Register" says "The dispute between the manufacturers of scissors and the grinders of them is likely to be attended with serious consequences. At a general meeting held last night at the Hotel, (the resolutions of which could not be got ready for this day's Register), it was agreed among other things to prosecute a certain number whom they supposed to have been principals in the scheme of turning out to effect an advance of wages. A subscription of several hundred pounds was entered into for that purpose. The scissors manufacture from this stoppage in the grinding is nearly at a stand."

On September 9th a meeting was held at the Cutlers' Hall for the purpose of carrying out the above-named object. Mr. Wood was one of a sub-committee appointed to give effect to the resolutions of the manufacturers. The result was that:

"Five poor honest grinders to prison they sent."

This only called forth more vindictiveness, Mather being the champion of the men.

In a subsequent number, the "Register" says "It would give us great pleasure to announce the settlement of this 'dispute,' as both parties must be suffering,— the one for want of money, the other for want of work."

It was stated before a committee of the House of Commons in 1833, "That combinations commenced in Sheffield in 1810, and before that time the masters and workmen lived together on the most perfect terms of good fellowship." This song entirely dissipates that notion. It is too late now to decide the merits of the strike, but it appears to have been like the modern practice of meeting one combination by another, instead

CHORUS

Then Haman he vowed that all Israel should die;
And Mordecai hang 'twixt the earth and the sky;
But though he on plunder and rapine was bent,
He never took discount at fifty per cent.

Then Haman sent forth that it was the king's word
For each tribe of Israel to die by the sword;
His breast that no mercy or clemency knew,
Thought he by their death all the Jews to subdue.
Bat "Hallamshire Haman," proud infernal elf,
For cruelty equalling Nero himself,
Who knew he must fall, should we rot in our graves,
He makes us pay discount for being his slaves.

This "Hallamshire Haman" keeps blacks at command,
To spread his dire mandates throughout the whole land,
Together they meet and their malice combine
To form a most hellish, infernal design.
On malice, on mischief, and tyranny bent,
Five poor honest[61] grinders to prison they sent;
Though nothing they had of these men to complain,
But not paying discount for wearing a chain.

He took a poor man to where justice is sold,
And mercy polluted for lucre and gold;
To ruin his family he was fully bent,
And fain he to Wakefield this man would have sent.
But while for revenge he thus cruelly sought,
In a snare of his own this proud Haman was caught;

---

of each party being left perfectly free.

[60] *Vide* Esther, chap. 3.

[61] See Sheffield Register, Sept. 24, 1790. Five scissors grinders were committed to Wakefield, four of them for 3 months, the other (Mordecai) for 4 months. The charge against them was refusing to take in their work after having it out more than eight days.

He dare not face justice, lest she should ordain
That he should pay back all his discount again.

This "Hallamshire Haman," proud infernal thing,
Expects the next year to be Hallamshire's King,
But proverbs assure us that those who would sip,
Shall find that much falls " 'twixt the cup and the lip."
So if his great master should send in the year,
And cite him at his dreadful court to appear,
In torments and flames he must certainly dwell,
And discount resound from the corners of—.

SONG XXVI.
SANCHO[62]

When Sancho was a raw-boned whelp,
   And lived in yonder jennel,
Although he snatched, the curs did yelp,
   And chas'd him to his kennel.
When but a little snarling pup,
   He thought himself most famous,
In that delusion he grew up,
   Both fool and ignoramus.

CHORUS

---

[62] This song, like the preceding one, satirises Mr. Geo. Wood, who was Master Cutler, in 1791-2. Sheffield at that time was supposed to be disaffected towards the Government. The "Rights of Man" being the text book of the Jacobins, Government issued a proclamation against seditious writings, evidently directed against Paine's work, though not naming it. The ministry of the day urged "the Magistrates to watch vigilantly all disaffected persons." Mr. Wood (in his official capacity) called a public meeting at the Town Hall, June 11, 1792, for the purpose of taking into consideration "The propriety of addressing His Majesty on his most gracious Proclamation." This meeting is forcibly described in the next song It is somewhat singular that the Master Cutler did not preside at the meeting.

See! how he flees in mad career,
With Mammon for his backer,
Grac'd with a firebrand at each ear,
And tail a flaming cracker.

Now purse-proud, soft, and ignorant,
  He instigates a faction,
Then tells us soldiers shall be sent
  To keep us in subjection.
Oft private interest needs a tool,
  To bring about oppression,
For that same end the red-hot fool
  Retains his old commission.

And daily flees, &c.

By Chesterfield he took his round,
  'Twas at the revolution,
And hunting in forbidden ground,
  They sought his execution;
But mercy interfered that day,
  Although he was convicted,
Which made presumption plumply say,
  "This proves he is elected."

Yet still &c.

In quest of game by foul demeans,
  A sacred place he riffled,
Where nine times twenty-five thirteens
  Were altogether stifled.
His dragon's tongue with fiery stream,
  Spued forth infernal slander,
Set all around him in a flame,
  Like some hot Salamander.

See! how he, &c.

His gilded god keeps all in awe,
  But speak and he'll indict you;
Approach his kennel, touch a straw,
  And doubtless he will bite you.
But if you speak of oil or blanks,
  Or mention whom he fleeces,
You instantly must shift your shanks,
  Or you'll be torn to pieces.

    For still he, &c.

Though he's attained to hoary hairs,
  His heart is dark and callous,
And doubtless soon will say his prayers
  Beneath some tree or gallows:
Then gladly for an iron suit
  The public will contribute,
The surgeons need not make dispute,
  For Sancho shall grace a gibbet,

    Nor longer fly, &c.

SONG XXVII
BRITONS, AWAKE[63]

Awake from your letharghy, Britons, awake,

---

[63] Mather again sang the popular feeling in this song. The Jacobins carried an amendment, by a great majority, against the combined power of the clergy and gentry. The "Register" in reporting the meeting, says "A plain man came forward and delivered an address calculated to point out the impropriety of the measure, which gave occasion to a very long if not a very temperate speech from the Rev. Mr. Russell," (Head Master of Dronfield Grammar School.) On the 13th instant, the promoters of the meeting called another at the Cutlers' Hall, of those persons who were "favourable to thanking his Majesty," when the following resolution was carried: "That an address be presented to his Majesty expressive of thanks for his late Royal Proclamation against 'Seditious Writings,' and that the meeting do esteem it their duty to give the utmost support in its power to the said Proclamation."

Your lives and your liberties all are at stake;
Why should you repose in security's arms,
When every moment's expos'd to alarms;
The powers of darkness afresh are enrag'd,
To work out your ruin they all are engaged.
See liberty banish'd! the clergy deprav'd!
Religion in sackcloth! the people enslaved!

Last Monday, if Beelzebub had not been chained
A most diabolical point he had gained,
He stretched the last link to collect a vile crew,
To render thanksgiving where stripes were most due.
He rallied his forces his cause to maintain,
At Bang-beggar Hall he assembled his train,
With teeth and nails sharpen'd soliciting power,
Like ferocious hell-hounds the poor to devour.

A fire engine pan when discharging the stream,
Those fiends represented when backing their scheme;
Their breath was so hot, made me stand in amaze,

    The parties who successfully carried the amendment at the first meeting were in attendance at this, but the meeting was what would now be called a "hole and corner meeting," it being called for those who *would sign the address*. This manoeuvre put the Jacobins out of court. On finding themselves duped, they again filled the Town Hall and called Mr. Gales to the chair. His conduct was animadverted upon at the meeting of the "Church and King" party, which called forth some explanations in the "Register" the following week. There appears from this ex-parte statement nothing objectionable in the conduct of the editor of the paper. The substance of his address was that having carried their amendment at the public meeting, they ought to allow those who differed from them in opinion to meet and express their own sentiments as they thought fit. Mr. Gales reminded the meeting that those who voted for the Amendment on the 11th inst. would not sign the address on the 13th.

    It is probable that an incident that took place when the meeting broke up rendered Mr. Gales more obnoxious than before. The majority present, as if to assert their principles, accompanied the chairman to his office in the Hartshead, singing Mather's song, beginning—

    "God save great Thomas Paine."

Expecting to see it break forth in a blaze;
Such infernal sulphur and sparks flew about,
Some coughing, some sneezing, some farting came out.
Declaring when they had recover'd their breath,
That Bang-beggar Hall was a hell upon earth.

Like Jericho's walls, the address tumbled down,
Which gave satisfaction to thousands in town,
But gave the vile crew both the cholic and gripes,
They all stood in need of old Brown's glister pipes.
When Russell discovered his scheme was made void,
Altho' a black hell-hound some thought he'd have dy'd,
An ague fit seized him, convulsions ensued,
And all the way home fire and brimstone he spued.

Old Brown,[64] with two faces, a popular tool,
That day filled the chair to keep order and rule;
His gilded deception threw dust in some eyes.
All could not descern him a fiend in disguise.
A vile proclamation pick'd up at hell's mouth,
That means to make libels or treason of truth—
They met to give sanction, but I must confess
I've seen a more excellent speech by an ass.[65]

SONG XXVIII
TRUE REFORMERS[66]

---

[64] Dr. Brown must have been denounced *simply as a tory politician*. He was a great benefactor to the Infirmary and the Charity Schools, and was Chairman of the Corn Committee in 1795. On August 22, in that year, a number of women wanted to draw the Dr. though the town in a carriage, which they took to the Cutlers' Hall for that purpose. This honour was declined, the Dr. observing "That it would invert the order of things and be ungallant." He died, deeply lamented, April 10, 1810.

[65] Numbers, chap. 22.

[66] The persons named in this song were the acknowledged leaders of the reform movement. Several of them became martyrs to their political opinions. Thomas Muir, Esq., a noble-minded patriot, was tried for

Come, ye patriots bold, whose affections are cold
   Towards tyrannical monsters' laws,
Let's true friendship display, and comem'rate the day
   That our brethren escap'd from their foes:

When the bloodhounds of state were most insatiate
   For the lives of brave Hardy and friends,
Heaven lent her kind aid to those mortals betray'd,
   And redeem'd them from ruffians and fiends.

Into ruin we sink, England's now on the brinks
   By its infernal wise men's exploits;
Swift destruction to all who our lives do enthrall
   And invade constitutional rights.

"sedition," on the 30th August, 1793, and after a trial of 18 hours was sentenced to 14 years' transportation. He made an eloquent address to the jury, and towards its conclusion he asked "What then is my crime ? Not the lending a relation a copy of Paine's works,—not the giving away to another a copy of a constitutional publication,—but my crime is for being a strenuous advocate for an equal representation of the people in the house of the people, for having dared to accomplish a measure by legal means which was to lessen the weight of their taxes and to put an end to the profusion of their blood. Gentlemen, from my infancy to the present moment, I have devoted myself to the cause of the people. *It is a good cause, it shall ultimately prevail, it shall finally triumph*" The Rev. J. R. Palmer was transported about the same time for a like period. The voice of Sheffield was heard on behalf of these patriots. On April 7, 1794, at a public meeting held on Castlehill, (Henry Redhead Yorke in the chair,) it was resolved "to present an address to the King, on behalf of Muir, Palmer, Skirving, Margarot, and Gerald, convicted of libels—to petition the King for the total abolition of slavery, and that no farther petitions be presented to the House of Commons on the subject of Reform." In the House of Commons, it was moved by Mr. Adams for an address to his Majesty, "to order the records of Muir's trial to be laid on the table." This was seconded by Mr. Fox, and supported by Sheridan and Mr. Grey, (Earl Grey of the Reform Bill), but such was the power of toryism that the motion was rejected by 170 votes against 32. Times have strangely altered since then. For a full account see "Howell's State Trials."

When arraign'd at the bar, Hardy shone like a star,
  Though opposed by the infamous Ross;
But alas, to be brief, his poor wife died with grief—[67]
  Ah, who can compensate his loss.

Consolation to Muir, may his heaven be secure—
Skirving's, Palmer's, Yorke's, Marg'rot's, and Paine's;
Let's not Gerrald forget, nor the least patriot,
  Whose characters admit of no stain.

'Twould be cruel to o'erlook Erskine, Gibbs, and H. Tooke,
  Who defeated their wicked design;
May Thelwall and the rest with good juries be blest,
  And their souls through eternity shine.

SONG XXIX
NORFOLK-STREET RIOTS[68]

---

[67] Montgomery, in the Iris, printed a few pathetic lines on the death of Mrs. Hardy, who died from anxiety concerning the fate of her husband.

[68] This song relates to a riot which took place in Norfolk street, on the 4th of August, 1795. The origin of the disturbance was trivial. A number of privates in Colonel Cameron's newly raised regiment refused to disperse after evening parade. The Col. remonstrated with his men, who alleged that part of their bounty money was withheld, besides some arrears in their pay. This circumstance caused numbers of people to assemble in Norfolk street, as Mather sung—
  "To see what meant the noise."
It is probable that the reports of the "Iris" and the "Courant" are tinctured with the political feelings of their respective editors.
The report of the liberal paper says "That Colonel Athorpe in a peremptory tone ordered the people instantaneously to disperse) which not being immediately complied with *a person who shall be nameless* plunged with his horse among the unarmed, defenceless people, and wounded with his sword men, women, and children promiscuously; the people murmured and fell back in confusion; the Riot Act was read: the people ran to and fro, scarcely one in a hundred knowing what was meant by these dreadful measures; when an hour being expired the Volunteers fired upon their townsmen with *bullets*, and killed two persons upon the spot: several others

Corruption tells me homicide
Is wilful murder justified,
A striking precedent was tried
In August, 'ninety-five,
When arm'd assasins dress'd in blue
Most wantonly their townsmen slew,
And magistrates and juries too
  At murder did connive.

---

were wounded, the rest fled on every side in consternation; the whole town was alarmed, and continued in a state of excitement all night long." Montgomery said that the coroner's jury would bring in a verdict of "justifiable homicide;" the event proved this. The article in the "Iris" is quite mild in comparison to this song, according to which Mather was an eye witness of the affair. Montgomery was prosecuted for a libel on the gallant Colonel Athorpe, and on the 21st of January, 1796, was fined £50 and sentenced to six months' imprisonment (his second) in York Castle, to give security for his good behaviour for two years, himself in £200, and two sureties in £50 each.

The "Courant" (the Tory paper) speaking of the Colonel's conduct says "Colonel Athorpe came up and prayed the people to disperse, but meeting a reception which indicated opposition he brandished his sword, and rode backward and forward amongst them without any military assistance: nor can I find by the most diligent search that there is any other ground for an assertion published in the "Iris" "That a person who shall be nameless plunged with his horse among the unarmed, defenceless people, and wounded with his sword men, women, and children promiscuously," than the *ipse dixit* of a simpleton who heard that another heard, that at one blow Col. Athorpe severed the head entirely from a child and cut its mother's breast off!!

It would be difficult now to decide the merits of this calamity. Sheffield was regarded as being disloyal. In 1793 a petition from a public meeting for parliamentary reform was rejected by the House of Commons for containing disrespectful expressions. The Volunteers of 1795 were supposed to be unfavourable to liberty, and consequently were not so popular as our present Volunteers are. (See song "Raddle-necked Tups.")

Perhaps the only person now (1861) living who was in the Norfolk street Riots *officially* is Mr. James Hinchcliffe, (better known as Jemmy Queer,) of Chapel street, Bridgehouses, (he was a drummer in the "Blues," or, as they were called in derision, "raddle neck'd tups," who paraded on the ground where St Marie's Church stands. He confirms the reports of both the newspapers in one respect, viz.: several of the

I saw the tragic scene commence;
A madman drank, without offence
Drew out his sword in false pretence,
   And wounded some more wise;
Defenceless boys he chased about,
The timid cried, the bold did shout,
Which brought the curious no doubt
   To see what meant the noise.

The gazing crowd stagnated stood
To see a wretch that should know good,
Insatiate thirst for human blood
   Like one sent from beneath;
This gave me well to understand
A sword pat in a madman's hand,
Especially a villian grand,
   Must terminate in death.

Volunteers being struck with stones while on parade; in fact he well remembers the cocked hat of Major Greaves being crushed by a large stone which was thrown into the parade ground. No one remembers more of the old worthies of Sheffield than Hinchcliffe: he says that when a lad he knew all the Jacobin songs, but that his father being a constable as well as a sergeant in the Volunteers, he would *not allow him* to sing them. To the memory of Jemmy Queer I am indebted for much information, and gratefully acknowledge the same. On the whole I incline to the belief that Col. Athorpe did ride among the rioters in the manner described in the "Iris." It was stated by the counsel for the prosecution of Montgomery that "the 'Iris" had long been the vehicle of abuse upon the Government of the country." And Col. Athorpe in his evidence on the trial says "that he had been dining with Earl Fitzwilliam, at Wentworth house… and that he rode from Rotherham as fast as he could possibly ride." It is probable that the gallant officer in the excitement of the moment might not be master of himself. The Colonel's horse died the next day!

    Messrs. Holland and Everett, the biographers of Montgomery say in a note at page 235, vol. 1, "We have heard Montgomery advert to the striking sentiment in the last two lines in the fifth stanza." The idea of the devil blushing is very poetical.

'Twas manifest in the event
That what the bloody tyrant meant
Was murder without precedent.
Though by injustice screened.
The "'Courant'"[69] may her columns swell,
Designing men may falsehoods tell,
Not all the powers of earth and hell
   Can justify the fiend.

This arm'd banditti, filled with spleen,
At his command, like bloodhounds keen,
In fine, to crown the horrid scene,
   A shower of bullets fired.
The consequence was deep distress,
More widows, and more fatherless,
The devil blushed and did confess
   'Twas more than *he* required.

Corruption cried for this exploit
"His worship shall be made a knight,
I hold his conduct just and right.
   And think him all divine."
Oppression need not fear alarms,
Since tyranny has got such swarms
Of gallant heroes bearing arms,
To butcher-grunting swine.[70]
The stones besmeared with blood and brains,

---

[69] The Tory paper, established November 10, 1793; died of inanition August 4, 1797.

[70] Burke's saying of the "swinish multitude" was often noted in Sheffield. The following lines are the introduction to a song called "The Swine," written by a native at this time:

> "We SWINE if I'm not far mistaken,
> These miseries ne'er can survive,
> They'll quarter us all to make *bacon*,
> Or eat us by inches alive."

Was the result of Robin's pains,
Surviving friends wept o'er the stains,
   When dying victims bled;
As Abel's blood aloud did call
To Him whose power created all,
Eternal vengeance sure must fall
   Upon his guilty head.

Ye wanton coxcombs, fops, and fools,
Aristocratic dupes and tools,
Subject yourselves to better rules,
   And cast away that badge.
Remember on a future day
Corruption must be done away,
Then what will you presume to say
   When truth shall be your judge?

SONG XXX
THE BRAWN[71]

Good people I pray you draw near,
   And I'll read you a riddle of mine;
It is of a brawn as you hear,
   Whose picture hangs up for a sign;
The sign it is fair to be seen,
   And to know where he lives you may lack,
It is down by the West-bar green,
   Where he hangs with his hull on his back.

This brawn he is vicious and stout,
   Two steps there go up to his hull,

---

[71] The Anglo-Saxon for Boar.
      This song satirises the "Host" of the Boar, (now the Blue Pig,) Spring Street. On the sign was painted a large picture of the above-named animal, to which Mather compares Mr. John Hawke, the landlord. John stood on little ceremony when his customers were drunk, but "He tumbled them neck and heels out, when with swillings their bellies were full."

Hell tumble you neck and heels out,
  When with swillings your belly is full.
I'd have you beware of his tushes,
  For I make no doubt as I'm told,
But some part or other he crushes,
  If once he does fairly lay hold.

I've heard people say very oft,
  A mechanic he was to be made,
But he was so peevish and soft.
  He never could master his trade,
At length being tired of his station,
  Resolved he was in his mind,
To travel from nation to nation,
  Till some better place he could find.

At Gib'he arrived at last,
  And by cheating poor soldiers there,
He gather'd up acorns so fast,
  They served him for many a year.
Being puff'd up with beggarly pride,
  And ill-gotten treasure in store,
He's lately come here to reside,
  And he lives where I told you before.

He has an old sow of his own,
  But she does not satisfy him;
So he ranges all over the town,
  A seeking some others to brim;
He at length found the gingerbread baker,
  And his substance upon her does spend;
He swears he will never forsake her,
  Until he has gained his end.

SONG XXXI
ELEGY ON B. CLAY, ESQ.[72]

---

[72] It is somewhat singular that Robert Clay, Esq., of Attercliffe, is the only gentleman in the neighbourhood who was eulogized by Mather. Mr. Clay

Hark! what mean yon piercing cries,
Throbbing breasts, and pensive sighs,
Death alas! has just removed
One by high and low beloved.

CHORUS

Attercliffe, thy loss deplore,
Clay, thy donor is no more.

Orphans lisp "our friend is dead,
By whose bounties we were fed;"
Widows cry "we're all undone,"
Whilst their eyes like fountains run.

CHORUS

Attercliffe, thy loss deplore,
Clay, thy donor is no more.

Tyrants live to tyranize,
Men of mercy scale the skies;
Mortals all combine this day,
To lament immortal Clay.

THE WIDOW'S PRAYER

O may his spirit sweetly rest
   With those exalted saints above,
Who doubtless are for ever blest
   By virtue of redeeming love;
Then will his bold bright soul give praise
   To Christ his Saviour's endless days.

---

died March 28, 1786, and was buried in the old chapel, Attercliffe. *The Widow's Prayer*, and the *Orphan's Lamentation* appear to belong to the same benevolent gentleman.

The Orphan's Lamentation

Within this gloomy silent cell
  My much lamented friend doth lie;
Since he a prey to reptiles fell,
  My weeping eyes have not been dry;
His liberal hand, alas, no more
  Can clothe and feed an orphan poor.

SONG XXXII
THE BLACK RESURRECTION[73]

---

[73] This song relates to the widening of Church lane, in 1785. The Local Register for that year says "The Church lane made wider by taking in a portion of the Churchyard, and removing a certain number of bodies and coffins." This led to some serious commotions on the part of the inhabitants. Places of sepulcher have been almost universally held sacred, and the feelings of our ancestors were entitled to respect. Mather no doubt sang the popular feeling in this song, where he denounced the conduct of the Vicar (Rev. James Wilkinson,) and Clergy. Viewing it in this utilitarian age we think our author unnecessarily severe. In questions concerning the living and the dead, should necessity require, the latter should give place. It would certainly be painful to Mr. Wilkinson to give up a portion of consecrated ground for secular purposes. He was not the person to stand in opposition to any movement calculated to benefit the moral or physical condition of his parishoners; and though disturbing the graves of departed friends would be painful to survivors, those feelings would be confined to that generation, while the benefits remain for all succeeding ages. A glance at Gosling's map of Sheffield will show the necessity for widening Church-lane. Perhaps the only written description of this part is to be found in a work published about 40 years ago entitled "The Contrast, or Improvements of Sheffield." In this work the author (James Wills,) describes the various improvements in Sheffield during the preceding 60 years in the rudest doggerel. The part under notice he thus describes:
> "Proceed then up Church lane, that poor narrow place,
> With wood buildings projecting 'twas quite a disgrace;
> The roofs nearly meeting, a dark dreary street,
> Might justly he styled 'the robber's retreat.' "

There is something original in this song. The lamentation of those whose bodies had been disturbed by the "Black Resurrection "is very

I lived for a series of years
   Not far from the toll of the bell,
My house they pull'd over my ears,
   And I was consign'd to my cell.
Before my remains were dissolved
   The BLACK RESURRECTION took place,
My troubles upon me revolved,
   Much to the *old serpent's* disgrace.

The strangers and paupers that slept
   With me in the peaceable clay,
Who much in affliction had wept,
   The *serpent* hath seized his prey;
For justice and mercy he pleads,
   Assuming an angel of light;
We see by his infamous deeds

---

striking. The first two lines in the last stanza are very poetical, and the whole piece displays a rich imagination: but surely to denounce the amiable Mr. Wilkinson as the "Old Serpent" was too severe. It is a singular coincidence that our church-yard has furnished a theme for two bards, and that both were brought up to the file trade. The poet "Laureate," of the Park Ward, (the late George Allen,) sung "*my nook in the Parish Church-yard*," on the occasion of that and other burial places in the town being closed by an "order in council," in 1857. For the gratification of those who have not seen the original I quote two verses:

> "In a nook in the parish church-yard
>   My wife and my children all lie,
> They're waiting beneath the green (?) sward,
>   Expecting my bones when I die."

> "I would if I could tell George Grey*
>   He played a ridiculous card
> When he *drove all the dead folks away*
>   From their nooks in the parish church-yard,"

Mr. Allen here displays not only originality but we may discover "The poet's eye in a fine frenzy rolling."

* Sir George Grey, the Home Secretary, who issued the order for robbing Allen of his "nook."

The widow he robs of her mite

Thus raised by his infernal power
   I went the old ruins to view,
I saw in the course of an hour
   Wide streets and high buildings all new,
And heard a lamentable cry
   Of many a serpent-stung friend,
Whose all had been sacrificed by
   That *black diabolical fiend.*

Did not his implacable spleen,
   Which ransack'd and tore up our graves,
Exhibit a tragical scene
   To gratify Beelzebub's slaves,
Whose interest it served to destroy
   Our mansions as well as remains,
To render *them* pompous and high
   That should be suspended in chains.

How striking to our weeping friends
   That saw us thus mangled and torn,
By ravishing hell-hounds and fiends,
   Who long stench of brimstone had borne:
Here was the extent of his sting,
   Whose power could no further encroach;
The tombs with his infamy ring
   To his everlasting reproach.

Although my detestable dust
   Be scattered thoroughout the whole globe,
I'll rest in an unshaken trust
   "To see my redeemer with Job;"
The serpent will then hang his head
   With his diabolical tribe,
When all their indictments are read,
   Which I'm at a loss to describe.

Not suffered to stay above ground,
   Nor yet in my grave to remain,
I'll watch till the trumpet shall sound,
   My ashes cast out of dead lane,[74]
Aud then re-ascend to my rest,
   Resume both my harp and my crown,
Enjoy the reward of the blest
   When all the black herd are gone down.

SONG XXXIII
RADDLE-NECK'D TUPS

Among some infernal productions
   Consistent with Norfolk-street news.
Black Cerberus pick'd up his instructions,
   And came a recruiting for blues.
My grandmother told me last winter,
   But hoped I'd her dotage excuse,
They were by a democrat printer
   Call'd "Raddle-neck'd Tups" and not blues.

Not blues, &c.

My name is Timothy Careless,
   I sprang from a vagabond Jew,
I'm subtle, blood-thirsty, and careless,
   Exactly the thing for a blue.
To fighting I am but a stranger,
   Its consequence I never knew,
I take to my heels when in danger,
   And just skulk away like a blue.
My thoughts in succession are evil,
   My clothes are both ragged and few,
Last week I shook hands with the devil,
   And then volunteer'd for a blue,

---

[74] The grave

Like him that leads up our banditti
   To Beelzebub I will be true,
I'll show no love, remorse, or pity,
   And that's just the part of a blue.

'Tis true we're the slaves of oppression,
   The sensible slaves to subdue;
While curs'd villany rides in procession,
   Protected by hell-hounds in blue,
The poor must all be kept under,
   Held down as it were with a screw,
The rich with impunity plunder,
   And boast of assassins in blue.

The fate of the *swine* we'll determine,
   Repeated insults they shall rue,
They think us detestable vermin,
   More fitted for halters than blue;
When tyranny offers a bounty
   The Norfolk-street feats well renew,
And slay all the pigs in the country
   That grunt at us, butchers in blue.

If I be convicted of murder
   A jury will pull me clean through,
They'll say "twas maintaining good order,"
   And tell me I am a true blue.
Mad Cerberus was our commander
   When Sorsby and Bradshaw we slew,[75]
We took him for great Alexander,
   He played such exploits in his blue.

But ah! if the French should invade us,
   How must we approach Pichegru?[76]
In Wharncliffe our chief man parade us,
   For none durst be seen in his blue.

---

[75] See song "Norfolk-street riots," Sorby & Bradshaw were shot there.
[76] The French General.

B—s—t in the hole of some badger,[77]
   I would raise an uncommon stew:
In like manner I durst lay a wager
   Would be every hero in blue.

Till brave San-Cullotes returned homewards
   We should not wear out many shoes;
The strongholds of foxes and polecats

---

[77] This a satire on the valour of the Sheffield independent volunteers, established April, 1794, and consisting of 590 men, under the command of the Earl of Effingham. In December, in the same year, Major Athorpe succeeded the Earl of Effingham as Lieut. Col. He retained his commission until October 31, 1799, when he resigned the command, which was again taken up by the noble Earl, Mather appears to have had great antipathy against Mr. Athorpe, both as a Magistrate and as Colonel of the volunteers. There is another song quite jubilant on the occasion of the Colonel resigning his commission. The chorus says:
   "Let all men living
   Join in thanksgiving,
   He's out of commission, boys, now, now, now"

In a small collection of Jacobin songs (now before me) printed in Sheffield, in 1797, there is a keen satire in two parts on a "volunteer." His inefficiency in his drill is thus set forth:
   When more than three months they'd this numskull been drilling,
   He handled his piece as a cow would a shilling;
   The commander exclaimed 'What the hell mast be done?
Such a blockhead I think ne'er supported a gun.' "

The hero of the piece, in order to acquire efficiency in his drill, resolved to practise at home when the rest of the family were locked in the arms of Morpheus. Poor Bill found a *broom*, and to his great delight performed his nocturnal exercise until he nearly knew *"his left hand from his right."* The head of the broom however by some mischance came off, and knocked down a number of pots from a shelf, which so perplexed this defender of his country that he was found next day in a woeful plight under the sacks in his father's malt house. His situation is thus described:

   "Next day came three fellows to fetch him to drill,
   Who sought high and low in the malt house for Will,

Would be sanctuaries for blues.
Should interest become a temptation,
I would, with my infernal crew,
Sell loyalty, sovereign, and nation,
And go to old Nick like a blue.

SONG XXXIV
NOTHING LIKE LEATHER[78]

> At length the old man pronounced loudly, 'I think
> He's got under the sacks, it is plain from the stink,'
> Then each man approached, stopping closely his nose,
> For they found he'd made *terrible work with his clothes*;
> As they could not convey him to drill on their backs,
> He in this situation is left in the sacks."

The songs from which this selection is taken have a strong political bearing, and were written by a young man who subsequently became known for his scientific attainments.

[78] In this song is exemplified the old saying "There is nothing like leather." Old men now say when they were lads they wore leather breeches, and were fed on sour oat cakes. Wills, the tailor, in the "Contrast," (before quoted,) page 18, says:

> "The church-going clothes of our Hallamshire lads.
> Coats twenty years old and their hair pat in pads,
> With strong buckskin breeches, and waistcoats of shag,
> No wonder they put so much money ith'bag.
> Striped pudding-poke nightcaps, worn all the week long,
> With broad buckles at shoes, both easy and strong."

If the clothing of our ancestors would endure twenty years' service Mather might well say there was nothing fit to compare with doe-leather breeches. Sheffield appears to have been famous for deer. After the funeral of Francis Earl of Shrewsbury, October 21, 1560, there was a grand dinner prepared, on which occasion the Hallamshire historian says "That among other things there were killed for the same feast fifty does and twenty-nine red deer." *Vide* Planter's Hallamshire, p. 57.

This song must have been composed about the beginning of 1790, from the allusion to the Prince of Wales wearing doeleather

All you that wear breeches, both women and men,
Attend to these verses, the fruit of my pen;
  With short introduction my story begins;
For beauty and service no stuff I declare
Was e'er manufactured that's fit to compare
  With doe-leather breeches, the best of two skins.

The tailor condemns them for sinister ends,
Because neither wages nor cabbage depends;
  Thus wronging his conscience he adds to his sins:
The mercer he skits them, I'll tell soon you why,
His craft is in danger, and suffers thereby:
For beauty and service no stuff I declare
Was e'er manufactured that's fit to compare
  With doe-leather breeches, the best of two skins.

Their natural colour (it is no way a lie;)
As black as a raven my skins I can dye,
  And colours in fact as the rainbow scarce wins;
The grave or the gay I can equally suit;
Make trial, my story no man will dispute;
For beauty and service no stuff I declare
Was e'er manufactured that's fit to compare
  With doe-leather breeches, the best of two skins.

The farmer commends them for wearing like steel,
The traveller likes them because they're genteel,
  And sings of their merit wherever he inns;
The Prince when at Wentworth and nobles also,
All made their appearance in neat foreign doe;
For beauty or service no stuff I declare
Was e'er manufactured that's fit to compare
  With doe-leather breeches, the best of two skins.

"inexpressibles" when on a visit to Wentworth House September 2nd, 1789. Earl Fitzwilliam gave a grand *fete* on the occasion, when about 40,000 persons were regaled in the park with meat and drink.

SONG XXXV
THE COCK-TAIL LADY[79]

Hague says to Beet, let's go ride the gray horse,
Come along then says Jack, tho' it is to my loss
Ball's supper'd up, and old Samuel's in bed,
Smiling Kate to entice us has drest up her head,
   Jem looks asquint,—to see powder in it,

---

[79] Furnace-hill is still called the Cock-tail by old people. The origin of the name does not appear, unless from its shape resembling the curved feathers in a cock's tail. The heroine of this song was the daughter of a publican, who lived in Furnace hill. I have been told by an old lady that 70 years ago she frequently saw the "Grand cock-tail lady," and that she was really a *smart young woman*, dressed in the highest style of fashion. There is force in the line:

"Cow-leather manners to strut in stuff shoes."

The fashion described in the song might well startle our ancestors, who often dressed in blue bed gowns. In a song written about the same time as this, the slighted lover says in true Sheffield dialect:

> " 'Two'r but last Shevild fair
> When we met, I declare,
> We put up at the sign o'the 'Crawn,'
> Tho luv'd me thaw sed,
> And a promise I made
> To buy thee a *new woolsey geawn*"

I am afraid that the homely dress of our maternal ancestors would have little charms in the eyes of modern sweethearts: neither is it desirable that the fair sex should be clothed as they were when this song was written. The head dress must have been of large proportions, because Mather says that some of the ladies had stolen the sounding board out of Ecclesfield church, to deck the upper part of their bodies. This song also exemplifies how commonly parochial offices descend from father to son.

The line:

"Tell Stringer, the clerk, he'll not miss his mark."

would apply to the Ecclesfield clerk (Matthew Stringer,) at this time. The honest indignation of the lady's father is finely described in the chorus: for example, these lines—

"Her bonnet balloon, I wish at the moon.

   Mammy to back it is commonly ready,
   Rivals who sit spending all their wit,
Turn out and fight for the grand cock-tail-lady.

Thus sung old Samuel, inspired by his cup,
The head of my daughter deserves blowing up;
Blow up her head,—with powder o'er spread,
   Her lappit caps and perfuming pomatum,
Her bonnet balloon I wish at the moon;
I say blow them up, for I mortally hate 'em.

Beet cry'd, it's wrong for a Derbyshire wench
To be powder'd and puff'd in the mode of the French,
Cow-leather manners to strut in stuff shoes
Is a notable crime, as you'll find in the news.
   At her swing glass her time she doth pass,
   And kicks at the wholesome advice of her daddy,
   The lin'-and-wool wheel may go the devil,
These are the scorns of the grand cock-tail lady.

On Sunday night I beheld smiling Kate,
Come shining along with a wonderful pate;
Greatly amazed at the sight I did stop,
I thought on her head was a spring table top,
   Beat better skill'd, —with laughter was fill'd,
   Seeing me struck with a head so unsteady,
   Replied it's a hat,—what think you of that,
Fool's pennies bought for the grand cock-tail-lady.

All thro' West-bar, strange enquiries were made
Who had darken'd their windows and doors with her head;
Some people said it was really a shame,
But the greater part wished it had been in a flame.
   Old Triggy cry'd, yonder's beggarly pride,
   Mounted on horse-back riding so heady;

    I say blow them up, for I mortally hate them."
   This feeling would find a response in the heart of many an indignant papa.

    She is running quick to get to old Nick:
Ride forward Kate, thou'rt the grand cock-tail-lady.

Warrants are granted in order to search
For the sounding board stole out of Ecclesfield church;
Sacrilege sure is a crime double dy'd
Yet 'tis here the result of this new fashioned pride;
   Fixed on a skull, deck'd with my arms full
   Of ribbons and gauzes, I beheld it already;
   Tell Stringer, the clerk, he'll not miss his mark
If he searches the house of the grand cock-tail-lady.

Three Rotherham girls I o'ertook on the road,
Who were wishing for hats that are now *a-la-mode*;
One said with ribbons and gauze I declare
I'll go deck our new tea-board, and shine at the fair;
   The next answered brief, our round table leaf
   I'll dress in like manner, and make it more shady;
   The third (more untow'rd) the church sounding board
She vow'd she'd steal to be like the grand cock-tail lady.

SONG XXXVI
SHOUT 'EM DOWN'S BARM[80]

---

[80] The narrow passage opposite the top of Townhead-street was known by the name of "Knock-'em-down alley." The theme of this song is Yorkshire ale, the virtues of which teetotallers may doubt. No subject, however, is more keenly controverted at the present day than the evils or benefits of alcoholic drinks. "Yorkshire Ale" was famed in song long before Burns wrote— "Inspiring bold John Barleycorn." "Giles Morrington "wrote a poem in praise of Yorkshire ale, which was published at York, 1697, in 12mo. In this work the names "knock-em-down," and "sting-o" are used as descriptives, and a long list of virtues is ascribed to ale. One of the most famous brewers in those days was a Madame Bradley. Whether her *recipe* has descended to Alderman Bradley I am not aware, though in October, 1857, this gentleman assured the burgesses of the Park Ward "That he brewed ale to warm the cockles of their hearts, and make them work better." Morrington thus describes Bacchus and his parliament sitting in judgement on Bradley's ale:

In Knock-'em-down Alley
I saw Tom and Sally;
Both lay sensless, as if they had been slain:
I could not help thinking
But they had been drinking
Too freely of smit'em, cut-throat, and tear-brain;
I told our old woman
Her drink was uncommon,

Madame Bradley's was the chief house then named,
There they must taste this noble ale so famed,
And nois'd abroad, in each place far and near;
Nay, take it Bradley, for strong ale and beer
Thou hast it loose, there's none can do so well,
In brewing ale thou dost all else excel."

This rare and curious poem is reprinted in Halliwell's "Yorkshire Anthology." Bacchus and his companions having drunk
"Till some could neither stand, go, sit, nor see,"
they declared,
"O Yorkshire, Yorkshire I thy ale it is so strong,
That it will kill us all if we stay long;
So they agreed a journey for to make
Into the South, some respite there to take;
But in short space again they said they'd come
And taste some more of this said Yorkshire "hum,"
It is so pleasant, mellow too, and fine,
That Bacchus *swore* he'd never more *drink wine.*

Mather, in this song, ascribes the potency of the liquor to its being worked with "Shout-'em-down's" barm. The "Norfolk Arms "public house, at the bottom of Norfolk street, was long called "Shout-'em-down's." It was then the "Owl," and kept by Mr. Michael Waterhouse. It was the rendezvous for several recruiting parties. The "Local Register" says that in 1793 there were thirty recruiting parties in the town. Mr. Waterhouse had been in the army, and seen much service: being an intelligent person his conversation proved almost as attractive as his ale, which must have been as famous as his "barm." Old Mr. Hinchcliffe says that when a lad he often "beat up" for recruits for "Shout-'em-down," who kept "The Hullett" (the Owl.) Mr. Waterhouse afterwards kept a public-house in Cheney square, (New Church street.)

Since two of her customers thus were done o'er;
   One quart of her stingo
   Would make the dumb sing-o,
The man that falls with it will never rise more.

CHORUS

*   The brewer excuses,*
*   For all these abuses.*
That range thro' the country exciting alarm;
*   'Tis not her resentment,*
*   Witchcraft, nor enchantment,*
But working her liquor with Shout-'em-down's barm.

   Last Sabbath day morning
   Will sure be a warning
To Turton, who felt the effects of our drink;
   He spent but one farthing,
   Reel'd into the garden,
And in a few moments was down in the sink;
   Knee-deep in the gutter,
   He made a strong flutter;
Like one that was drowning, he catch'd by the edge;
   If timely assistance
   Had been at a distance,
His church must have been overhead in the sludge.

   John Hallam, last summer,
   Who took a fall brimmer
Of old hock and knock-'em-down, instantly fell;
   Ah! what can the matter be?
   If he no better be,
Justice will grant no more licence to sell;
   Some strong Taylor's brandy
   We bottled last Monday;
On Tuesday, like shots all the corks took their flight,
   With much circumspection,

One took a direction,
Twas found below Masbro' on Saturday night.

   Whoever engages
   Spitfire and outrageous,
I tell them, lest I should my friends disoblige,
   Must dread an explosion,
   And handle with caution
Those vessels which burst like bombshells in a siege;
   Should Wainwright and Rowley,
   Dame Hoyland unweildly,
Brown, Carnelly, Hartley, Eyre, Handley, and Steel,
   All burst on the gantry,
   And o'erflow the country,
The works on the Don must the consequence feel.

   One morning young Nelly
   Came with her big belly,
Requesting a bottle against she lay in;
   Soon as she departed
   Behold how she started,
When out flew the cork, like the crack of a gun,
   As swift as an arrow
   It kill'd a cock sparrow,
A crow and a swallow, (if 'tis not a lie,)
   Astonish'd each neighbour,
   Threw Nell into labour,
And brought down a wild goose three hundred yards high

SONG XXXVII
THE BLIND FIDDLERS[81]

---

[81] Sheffield seems to have been famous for its blind fiddlers. Blind Stephen was quite a character, and possessed a large share of broad humour. The "Q in the Corner," in Paradise square, was a famous resort for fiddlers. The landlord, Samuel Goodlad, claimed the right to play the first fiddle on all public occasions, and used to boast that he got all new tunes from London before any one in Sheffield. This was probably true, because Mr. and Mrs.

Last market day even,
John Gibbons, blind Stephen,
And two other fiddlers that never could see,
They fought battle royal,
An hour by the dial,
Before that each party'd consent to agree,
The landlady cries out,

Goodlad had the entire management of the "Assemblies"—those fashionable gatherings of the *elite* of Sheffield, in the Assembly Booms, Norfolk-street (the Council Hall). On one occasion Samuel performed a selection of *new* music for the gratification of his customers, some of whom put blind Stephen in a sack, and carried him to the "Q," where he heard the mellifluous music of "mine host," who boasted after the performance that no fiddler in Sheffield could play that particular tune, which he only obtained the day before. While some of the company were congratulating Samuel, others carried out the sack and liberated Stephen from durance. He soon made his appearance with his fiddle, and wished to play for the amusement of *his friends*. On being asked if he could play the same tune *that only Mr. Goodlad knew*, Stephen declared that he could, *better than any man in Sheffield*. The landlord being positive that Stephen did not know it, offered to fiddle him for a "leg of mutton and trimmings" if he would play first. The offer was accepted, and Stephen was declared the victor, to the astonishment of his competitor, who greatly wondered where his rival got the tune. In due time the supper was prepared and ample justice done to it. But as the immortal Tam O'Shanter found it necessary to ride home, though he had to pass the haunted ruins of Kirk Alloway at the midnight hour, it was equally necessary for Stephen to go home, though he had to pass the parish church-yard at the same witching time. Stephen said he was not afraid of *seeing* a ghost; but as it was a dark night he asked if the kind-hearted hostess would lend him a *lantern*. This was a favour she could not deny. She told the servant girl to get one, and put a good light in it. Thus equipped, the jovial fiddler set off to Pinstone-lane; but he had scarcely got up the steps which led into the church-yard (it was a thoroughfare then, and not pallisaded) when some of the company asked Mrs. Goodlad why she lent a lantern to a blind man? She quickly bade the girl run after him and fetch it back, as the thing would be known all over the town. When the maid overtook Stephen and demanded the lantern, he refused to give it up, because Dame Goodlad had lent it him to go home. The girl said that a lantern was useless to a blind man, on which Stephen laughed, and said, "Does tha think I borrowed it for me sen? Tell thy

They'll knock all their eyes out,
A speech by a bystander not to be bore.
So down Sykes did toss her,
And laid the sack across her,
And there she remained till the battle was o'er.

SONG XXXVIII
GOD SAVE GREAT THOMAS PAINE[82]

God save great Thomas Paine,
His "Rights of Man" to explain
    To ev'ry soul.
He makes the blind to see
What dupes and slaves they be,
And points out liberty,
    Prom pole to pole.

Thousands cry "church and king"
That well deserve to swing,
    All must allow:
Birmingham blush for shame,

---

mistress that there are so many drunken folks in the streets, and if one knocked me down and smashed my fiddle I should be ruined. I am much obliged to her for the lantern, and although I can't see *other folks can.*"

    On the 3rd of May, 1810, six resident blind musicians had a benefit concert at the "Assembly Rooms." *Vide* Local Reg., p. 124

[82] This song, composed to the tune of the national anthem, was a favourite with the Jacobins. It will be remembered that it was sung at the close of a meeting in the town ball,—(see song 28.) The last verse shows the strong feeling that existed in those times. Paine, as politician, had great faith in democracy; but the experience of the French revolutions of 1703 and 1848 has not realized Paine's anticipations. The present disorganized condition of the United States is little calculated to spread democratic ideas. Paine attributed the miseries of mankind to bad government, and, therefore, sought for change. The greatest reform, and the one best calculated to elevate the people, would be a social and *moral* reformation. Let every man determine to reform *one*, and then it will be unnecessary for politicians to seek "organic changes."

Manchester do the same,
Infamous is your name,
  Patriot's vow.

Pull proud oppressors down,
Knock off each tyrant's crown,
  And break his sword;
Down with aristocracy,
Set up democracy,
And from hypocrisy
  Save us good Lord.

Why should despotic pride
Usurp on every side?
  Let us be free;
Grant freedom's arms success,
And all her efforts bless,
Plant thro' the universe
  Liberty's tree.

Facts are seditious things
When they touch courts and kings,
  Armies are rais'd,
Barracks and bastiles built,
Innocence charged with guilt,
Blood most unjustly spilt,
  Gods stand amaz'd.

Despots may howl and yell,
Tho' they're in league with hell
  They'll not reign long;
Satan may lead the van,
And do the worst he can,
Paine and his Rights of Man
  Shall be my song.

SONG XXXIX
THE GUINEA CLUB FEAST[83]

All we undermentioned have jointly agreed
To banish contention and discord with speed,
As friends to unite, and be nobly employ'd
In tipping off bumpers to loosen our hides;

Here's Pickering and Cooper, and Barber and Might,
Have made an agreement to drink the whole night,
Here's Sutton sits cross-leg'd clapping his breast,
To loosen their hides at the guinea club feast.

CHORUS

Then fill up a bumper and let it go round,
Why should a stark hide or a niggard be found?
May Bacchus's children have flowing spring tides,
And humming strong liquor to loosen their hides.

Here's Litton and Spencer, and Siddall and Sykes,
Foul weather in harvest, which no farmer likes,
Here's Mather and Dickson, Rhodes and Davenport,
Will loosen their hides, for they're lads of that sort;
Here's Colley and Hawley, and Epworth also,
Here's Richardson, Bayster, and Beet, we all know,

---

[83] No person can thoroughly understand the working classes, unless he associate with them in the manufactories or in their festivals. In this song Mather sings the glories of a "Guinea club feast," and names numbers of his friends who mean to "loosen their hides" at it. He slyly names some of the more devoted, who:

"Will tarry to-morrow to polish the bones."

Such persons are not yet without representatives. It is on such occasions when the thoughts, prejudices, and feelings of the workmen may best be known. A "leg of mutton and trimmings" won at quoits or at cribbage afford a fine opportunity for knowing the secret thoughts of the artizans, especially when they get "fou."

Here's Stephenson, Haley, and Gough, till deceas'd,
Will loosen their hides at the guinea club feast.

There's Burley and Furniss, tho' civil and dry,
Will tip up their buckets to heighten their joy;
Here's Holland and Lenton, and Whalley besides
Will have no objection to loosen their hides;

There's Anderton, Ashmore, friend Oxley, and Jones,
Will tarry to-morrow to polish the bones:
Here's Greaves and the Bishop confirming each guest
That's got a loose hide at the guinea club feast.

Altho' 'tis gone twelve, push the tankard about,
We sons of old Bacchus think it scorn to give out,
Go fetch up a barrel, let the bung be destroyed,
And never submit till we've loosened our hide;

In love and true friendship we mean to conclude,
And drink all the liquor our friend has got brew'd,
We'll drain every barrel, from biggest to least,
To loosen our hides at the guinea club feast.

SONG XL
THE NETHER GREEN LAD[84]

The Nether-green lad[85] had a spark in his throat,

---

[84] Nether-green, near Ran-moor.

[85] The Nether-green lad seems to have been a "true toper" in the popular acceptation of that term. "To dance, drink, and sing," were considered essential qualifications. His tunes were Mather's "Sancho," "Bang-beggar," and "Cock-tail." These were very popular fifty years ago. In no portion of society have greater improvements been made than amongst our artizans, especially in their drinking customs. Thirty years since drunkenness was very common on Sunday mornings. I personally knew one of my own trade stroll half seas over into a Wesleyen chapel one Sabbath day. The potency of the drink, combined with the loss of rest the previous night,

The ocean he drinks makes the landlady's note;
  Begot by old Bacchus, he calls him his dad;
His tenets he follows by day and by night,
In tipping a bumper he's exactly right,
He'll dance, drink, and sing, like a toper true-born,
And scorns to give out until three in the morn,
  Then goes reeling home like a Nether-green lad,
Who ne'er forgets tol de rol, tol de rol la.

Sancho, "Bang-beggar," or else "Cock-tail reel,"
He sings elevated astride of a stile,
  Regardless of highwayman or a footpad.
No sooner at home but he tumbles up stairs,
To keep a clear conscience he whistles his prayers,
Then tells them to lay a green sod at his head,
This motto inscribed on his tomb when he's dead,
  "Here lie the remains of a Nether-green lad!"
Who ne'er forgot tol de rol, &c.

SONG XLI
THE JUSTASS[86]

---

soon sent him to sleep, and his loud snoring disturbed the congregation. The chapel keeper roused him and requested him to leave the place. On recovering his consciousness he heard the voice of the preacher, and exclaimed, "He's beginning agean, let me hear t'other bit."

[86] I cannot ascertain whom Mather meant by the "Son of a baker who was made a just-ass." I have no doubt that our bard was strongly prejudiced against the whole bench of county magistrates, who sat each Tuesday to dispense law. The last few years of the eighteenth century were chequered by war and famine, as well as a discontented population. The duties of the magistracy were onerous, and doubtless mistakes were often made in the administration of the law; but surely no one deserves the fate Mather awards to his just-ass. *Apropos* to the subject of Justices of the peace, there is an anecdote related of the Rev. Charles Chadwick, sen., the vicar of Tinsley. Mr. Chadwick was headmaster of the Sheffield grammar school, as well as vicar of Tinsley. For the efficient discharge of both duties he kept a horse, and such a one as was no disgrace to his owner. On one occasion Mr. C. was riding from Tinsley (where his duty called him,) to the school at Town-head cross. As he was riding past the old Cutlers' hall, the

When poverty puts off her habit of rags
She quickly turns tyrant and boasts of her bags:
'Tis always the case with the dung-hill bred train,
To give the community cause to complain:
The poor are oppress'd by their infamous deeds,
For what they take from them their luxury feeds.
I'll tell you an instance will wonder surpass,
The son of a baker is made a just-ass.

One Tuesday, behind a green table I saw
A grand ignoramus currupting the law,
I thought to myself 'twas a desperate case
To see a mule sit in a magistrate's place;
For want of a right cultivation at school
He acted like tyrant, and madman, and fool.
I ask'd what irrational rascal that was,
And found 'twas a baker's son turned a just-ass!

It was not by merit he rose from the mire,
Altho' he arriv'd at the pitch of a squire;
A wealthy old miser this upstart may thank,
Who rais'd him from indigence to this high rank.
It would be more proper for such a blackguard
To govern wild creatures, or be a bear-ward,
Than hector in court, while the men of his class
Spite the son of a baker turn'd to a just-ass.
He formerly travell'd the streets crying rolls,
With both stocking heels out, and shoes wanting soles;
But now the poor vagrant he'll send to knock hemp,
Forgetting his pedigree was of that stamp.
The people of Yorkshire will merrily sing
When upon a gibbet the rascal shall swing;

---

magistrates were leaving their professional duties, when one of them called out "Here's Mr. Chadwick riding a *fine blood horse*, while his Master, with more humility, was contented with an *ass*." The rev. gentleman rejoined that "Your worship forgets that asses are *scarcer now* than at the time of which you speak." "How is that?" exclaimed his worship. "Why, because government get all they can to make justices of!"

Jack Ketch is desirous to handle the brass,
For hanging the baker's son turned a just-ass.

SONG XLII
THE OWL'S COMMISSION[87]

Last Tuesday, in the afternoon,
I took a ramble up the town,
Where numbers told me very soon
   The owl was in commission;
The more's the pity, I replies,
That such a wretch should tyrannize,
The jury will be deemed unwise
   For granting him commission.

They say 'twas done for this intent,
To keep the parish from expense,
Which would have been the consequence
   Of his distressed moaning;
Ere long a halter he will stretch,
While in the presence of Jack Ketch,
Who quickly will the halter stretch,
   That Tyburn may cease groaning.

SONG XLIII
HE'S OUT OF COMMISSION, BOYS

Now I've struck straight with neighbour Bob,[88]

---

[87] This song, like several other of Mather's, reflects on one of the magistrates, under the title of the "Owl." I cannot discover whom our author meant. It was probably Bacon Frank, Esq., a county magistrate of rather strong tory opinions. The last four lines exemplify an opinion then prevalent about the expediency of hanging. Old men now frequently say "there wants a hanging day."

[88] Mather most unrelentlessly pursues Colonel Athorpe. The cause was probably owing to his zeal in supporting the government of the day. Pitt,

And more of the infernal mob,
No longer with them I'll contend,
But leave them all for the devil to mend,
Though that busy insulting fiend,
Satan's agent, shall not be screened,
    Who maliciously,
    And most viciously,
  Seeks our ruin, we must each allow:
    Let all men living
    Join in thanksgiving,
He's out of commission, boys, now, now, now.

Last Easter, from Norfolk street Arms,
In King-street, Sheffield, strange alarms
Were circulated through this town,
When pulling this proud monster down,
There were present some trusty friends,
Whom we never can make amends,

---

the great minister, (who had been an ardent reformer,) had become eminently conservative. His whole energies were bent on humbling the French. To accomplish this object money was essential, and as Chancellor of the Exchequer Pitt's Financial policy was unpopular with those ardent politicians who gloried in the French Revolution. As free discussion was not allowed by the government, the opinions of the disaffected found expression in political songs; and in this class of literature Sheffield was famous. In the "Gallantly Show" the writer (a native) says:

> "Next you see at every dainty,
> *Billy* with his colleagues set,
> Yearly spending MILLIONS twenty,
> To pay off the nation's debt,
> While the poor by wicked laws, sir,
> Lose the uses of their *jaws*, sir,
> They are gorging at their case, sir,
> Just like maggots in a cheese, sir.

In this style the "Showman "reviews the policy of the government of the day, and these satires no one more desired to suppress than Mr. Athorpe. Hence the joy of Mather on Col. A. resigning his commission.

    Whose fidelity
    Brought tranquillity
  To this suffering town I vow,
    Let all men living
    Join in thanksgiving,
He's out of commission, boys, now, now, now.

This owl, or agent of old Nick's,
For divers base and subtle tricks,
Was undertook to be cashier'd:
And thanks be prais'd, the point was clear'd,
The powers of darkness did contend,
And plead for their infernal friend,
    But morality
    This black quality
  Quite defeated, they best know how:
    Let all men living
    Join in thanksgiving,
He's out of commission, boys, now, now, now.

Thus from a vast exalted height
He is brought down in a woeful plight;
Instead of hunting Linnen's stag,
He may procure himself a bag,
No longer must the wretch intrude,
His claws are cut his power subdued,
    And calamity,
    Want, and extremity
  Stamped upon his infernal brow,
    Let all men living
    Join in thanksgiving,
He's out of commission, boys, now, now. now,

SONG XLIV
WATKINSON AND HIS THIRTEENS[89]

---

[89] This, perhaps the most popular of Mather's songs, must ever be interesting from its historical associations. It shows the state of feeling existing between labour and capital more than seventy years ago. At the

That monster oppression, behold how he stalks,
Keeps picking the bones of the poor as he walks,
There's not a mechanic throughout this whole land
But what more or less feels the weight of his hand;
That offspring of tyranny, baseness, and pride,
Our rights hath invaded and almost destroyed,
May that man be banished who villainy screens:
Or sides with big Watkinson with his thirteens.

---

present day workmen imagine that they have greater difficulties to contend with than at any previous period. This satirical song displays no very amicable feeling between master and man. I can never forget the impression made on my mind when a boy on hearing it sung by an old cutler. This event happened on a "good saint Monday," during a "foot ale" which was drank in the workshop. After the singer had "wet his whistle" he requested his shopmates to assist in chorus, and then struck off in a manly voice, laying strong emphasis on the last two lines in each stanza, at the conclusion of which he struck his stithy with a hammer for a signal, when all present joined in chorus with such a hearty good will that would have convinced any person that *they felt* the "odd knife" would have been well employed in dissecting Watkinson's "vile carcase." The *popular* opinion is that Watkinson was a "screw," and the *first* master who compelled his men to make thirteen for a dozen. It is further alleged that this song heart-broke him. This appears to have some support from the song "Watkinson's Repentance," one verse of which shows that the "gods of the gallery "sang him out of the theatre. Jonathan Watkinson resided in Silver-street, and was one of the principal manufacturers of his day. He was master cutler in 1787, and one of the thirty-nine subscribers of £100 each for the erection of the Tontine Hotel, which occupied the site of the Market Hall, and was opened 1785. How far the conduct of Mr. Watkinson merited Mather's denunciations cannot now be satisfactorily established. I have heard several old workmen say that he was a master who paid a *good price* for his labour, and was a kind-hearted man. If money had been his god I scarcely think he would have died broken-hearted, because nothing sears the heart more than the love of money. Chaucer's Friar, to get money, always preached from the text "Radix malorum est Cupiditas." I cannot ascertain when Watkinson died. He was living in 1790, because the "Register" for February says "An attempt to rob his house was frustrated by one of his daughters. This led to the contemplation of establishing night watchmen for the neighbour hood." He was dead, however, in Dec., 1791. Another account, and not an improbable one, I derived from an old lady who personally knew Mr. Gales, Ebenezer Rhodes, Sylvester, Montgomery, Nanson, and

CHORUS

And may the odd knife his great carcase dissect,
Lay open his vitals for men to inspect,
A heart full as black as the infernal gulph,
In that greedy, blood-sucking, bone-scraping wolf.

This wicked dissenter, expelled his own church,
Is rendered the subject of public reproach:
Since reprobate marks on his forehead appear'd,
We all have concluded his conscience is sear'd:
See mammon his God, and oppression his aim,

---

others, who met in "Billy Hill's" parlour, (the Bull Inn, Wicker,) to discuss political and social topics, her husband being one of the party. Her account of the origin of "thirteens" is that during Watkinson's year of office some of the manufacturers complained of workmen keeping the odd materials as perquisites, (a grinder's dozen being fourteen, while horn, wood, and hone scales were thirteen.) To stop this system of *appropriation* the respectable masters desired the workmen to make thirteen and *be paid for them*; but that others, more unscrupulous, only paid for twelve. But the manufacture of cutlery being a monopoly Watkinson only acted in his official capacity as the head of the corporation. The resolutions of that body would be officially signed by the master cutler, upon whom fell the popular displeasure. This version is somewhat borne out by the fact that the Cutlers' statement (1810) still recognises *twelve* to the dozen, though fourteen are usually made. Some of the trade customs are very old, many things being sold by the "great hundred;" and I have heard Alderman Fisher say how he used to be puzzled when he first entered his father's warehouse. He had been taught at school that *twelve* dozen were one gross, but in practice he found that he had to count *thirteen* dozen scales for a gross. The question of "What is a dozen?" yet admits of doubt. In the *Independent* of March 30th, 1861, will be found a case in point, brought before the Mayor, (H. Vickers, Esq.,) and J. J. Smith, Esq. Richard Woodhead summoned Messrs. W. and S. Butcher for 13s. 5½d., being the difference in price, not between "twelves and thirteens," but between *twelves* and *fourteens*. Evidence was given on both sides, and the magistrates dismissed the summons, the endorsement being as follows "We are of opinion that the word 'dozen' in the agreement means fourteen knives for 7s. 8½d."

Hark! how the streets rings with his infamous name,
The boys at the playhouse exhibit strange scenes
Respecting big Watkinson with his thirteens.

And may, &c.

Like Pharoah for baseness, that type of the de'il.
He wants to flog journeymen with rods of steel,
And certainly would, had he got Pharoah's power,
His heart is as hard, and his temper as sour;
But justice repulsed him and set us all free,
Like bond-slaves of old in the year jubilee.
May those be transported or sent for marines
That works for big Watkinson at his thirteens.

And may, &c.

We claim as true Yorkshiremen leave to speak twice,
That no man should work for him at any price,
Since he has attempted our lives to enthral,
And mingle our liquor with wormwood and gall;
Come Beelzebub, take him with his ill-got pelf,
He's equally bad, if not worse than thyself;
So shall every cutler that honestly means
Cry "take away Watkison with his thirteens."

And may, &c.

But see foolish mortals! far worse than insane,
Three-fourths are returned into Egypt again;
Altho' Pharoah's hands they had fairly escaped.
Now they must submit for their bones to be scraped;
Whilst they give themselves and their all for a prey
Let us be unanimous and jointly say,
Success to our Sovereign who peaceably reigns,
But down with both Watkinson's twelves and thirteens.

And may, &c.

SONG XLV
BANG BEGGAR[90]

Young Lurk keeps a throstle whom nature has taught
A song which exceeds all conception or thought,
Too high for a letter-learned scholar to reach,
Yet, speaking with grace, I've attained a short sketch.
Last week when poor Will had his flogging receiv'd,
The bird lower'd his feathers apparently griev'd,

---

[90] This, like the proceeding song, alludes to Watkinson. The term "Bang-beggar's Hall "strongly expresses the dislike of the writer to judicial proceedings. The administration of justice should be above suspicion, justice is represented as blind, that both rich and poor may be unknown to her. The second stanza represents Watkinson sending an apprentice to prison for "crying thirteens." At the close of the last century the apprentices found almost constant employment for the magistrates. In fact the apprentices at that time were bound to the *masters*, who formed a society for recovering runaway apprentices. It was not until after the amendment of the Act, 21st James I, in 1791, that *workmen* were allowed to take apprentices. This exclusive system is yet the custom in some branches of the Sheffield trades. All saw makers, even workmen's sons, are appprenticed to the masters, and in the file trade each employer is entitled to have two.

It wept for a while with head under its wing,
Then, as the ghost renders it, thus it did sing.

CHORUS

At Bang-beggar's hall, in a Bang-beggar's cage,
To sing the Bang-beggar, tho' Bang-beggar rage,
A Bang-beggar's bird was ne'er heard from a bush,
To sing the Bang-beggar, like Bang-beggar's thrush.

I've sung loud two summers, till autumn came on,
Not hinting one crime that my master had done,
But finding it sin to connive at his ways,
I'll let out the cat, though she should end my days:
He seiz'd a poor lad they call Nottingham Will,
For crying thirteens, who thought it no ill;
Four days kept him starving amidst gloomy scenes,
Then banished and flogg'd him for crying thirteens.

When he wrought at cutling mere twelves made him sick,
And doubtless thirteens would have caus'd him to pick;
He joined the tame army, starve rather than work,
But getting disbanded they've made him Young Lurk.
He lurks for his madams, but these cost him pence,
Then seizes a tramper to pay the expense:
The premium got up for poor Will in his tears
Paid off Butter-Poll what was due in arrears.

Behold how he swells like a man of renown,
Tho' scorn'd and detested by most of the town.
In dignity far below ragman or sweep,
None should, save a hangman, his company keep;
But ignorance prompts him to swagger and prate,
Believing himself to be chief magistrate;
Unless the cat eat me I will not refrain
To sing the Bang-beggar till autumn again.

At Bang-beggar's hall, &c.

SONG XLVI
WATKINSON'S REPENTANCE[91]

At length this old Wolf to repentance is brought,
Who a long time in Sheffield hath wandered about,
A large blackguard snatch of late he hath made,
To pull down the prices of the cutlering trade.

CHORUS

But he gets well remember'd what a rogue he has been
In extending dozens from twelve to thirteen.

This is full repentance and a lamentable tale,
I had rather been broken and sent to the jail
Than heard such a scandal be sung thro' the town,
That the name of great Watkinson doth pull prices down.

It is every night when I go to my rest,
My conscience doth constantly pierce thro' my breast,
I seldom can sleep, but I constantly dream
I hear thousands shouting "I will have thirteen."
Once I was walking the street up and down,
The most that pass'd by me spoke with a frown,
Singing "there goes old Watkinson who hath lost his brain,
And never must recover his senses again."

One night to the play I happened to go,
But I could not rest long, they troubled me so,

---

[91] Mather's vindictiveness still pursues Watkinson. If there be a crime unpardonable in the opinion of Sheffield artizans, it is pulling down the price of their labour. There is no mistaking the author's meaning. He does not express himself ambiguously. A novice would understand the chorus, or the last line of the song. The fifth verse describes an incident that really happened. A relative of mine told me that when he was an apprentice his master related the circumstance of the master cutler giving a "bespeak" at the theatre. On his arrival Mather, from the gallery, "led off" "Watkinson and his thirteens," the "gods" vociferating the chorus until the master cutler retired.

For before in the play-house long time I had been,
The whole gallery shouted "I will have thirteen."

Come all Sheffield masters, take warning by me,
For fear you should share the same fate you see,
And never attempt poor men's bones for to scrape,
Who daily do labour for all that they do get.

SONG XLVII
TAPE ALLEN[92]

Some say Tape Allen is not to be a gunner,
  His head is so lofty the clouds it divides;
Others they say he'll make a special runner,
His legs are so long, that he takes such great strides,

> Some have got a notion,
> He'd stride across the ocean,
> Like Collossus
> When he crosses
>   The extensive seas.
>
> Then why should he refuse
> To go and bring us news
>   From America,
> When he could in one day
>   Set out from home,
>   Both go and come,
> With very much ease ?

SONG XLVIII
THE THANKSGIVING[93]

---

[92] Jemmy Queer says that Tape Allen was a very tall grenadier, who spent some time in Sheffield recruiting.

[93] It is very probable that Mather was once a Methodist, and this and the following piece show much of the phraseology of the early Wesleyans. The

Now peace to Britain is restor'd,
And George our king has sheath'd his sword,
The Prince of Peace should be ador'd
   By every mortal living.
Let all that breathe the vital air
Acknowledge His paternal care,
His love towards this land declare,
And give praise,—all their days,
   Worthy of true thanksgiving.

Since by transgression Adam fell,
Each man is born an heir of hell,
His fallen nature will rebel
   Throughout all generations.
The world through wickedness was drown'd,
Save eight who in the ark were found;

---

thanksgiving was written to commemorate the peace between Great Britain and the United States. This event gave general satisfaction to the inhabitants of Sheffield. The commencement of hostilities between Great Britain and her colonies, in 1775, according to the "Local Register" for that year, "created much alarm in the town, particularly among the merchants and factors, who during the last fifteen years had opened a trade to Philadelphia, Boston, and other places. At a later period the Register states that "the American war was the subject of complaint amongst masters and workmen, many of the latter, notwithstanding they were unemployed, were paid their weekly wages, in the hope that the ministry would conclude a peace with the United States. Several masters engaged in the plated manufacture advanced more than £100 to individual workmen." These surely were the times when silversmiths drank *wine* with their employers, and refused to sit in company with *cutlers and grinders*. I am afraid that the class of workmen named would find it difficult *now* to obtain credit for half the sum. Hostilities ceased between the contending parties April 17, 1783 and was ratified by congress January, 1784. The news, however, did not arrive in Sheffield until the 15th July that peace was proclaimed at the Royal Exchange, London. What tardy travelling! We obtain the news from Washington now in about as many days as it took months then. In Sheffield it was a true thanksgiving day. At *present* we could all join in the concluding prayer of the thanksgiving.

Gomorrah and the cities round
Were overturn'd,— altho' Lot mourn'd,
They were with fire and brimstone burn'd
  For their abominations.

Distresses from an enemy,
As well as each calamity,
We read in sacred history
  Were all the fruits of sinning.
View Adam when in Paradise,
Who in his Maker did rejoice,
And did with an unfeigned voice
Laud his name,—Eve the same,
Until the serpent wrought their shame,
  Lo! here was war's beginning.

The heart of man is still deprav'd,
And by infernal lusts enslav'd,
And Satan's image is engrav'd
  Until he is converted;
Make this a true thanksgiving day,
When all with one accord shall say
"The Lord incline our hearts to pray,"
And increase love and peace;
Then surely wars will ever cease,
  And Satan be deserted.

SONG XLIX
REPENTANCE[94]

With a sorrow for sin

---

[94] I was much struck once with hearing a venerable local preacher among the Wesleyans repeat this "hymn," particularly pointing out the evangelical truth as well as the poetic beauty of the third verse. On enquiring if he knew whose it was he said that when young the hymn was a favourite with his class leader.

Let repentance begin,
Then conversion of course will draw nigh,
   But till wash'd in the blood
   Of a crucified God,
We shall never be ready to die.

   And that we may succeed,
   Let us haste with all speed
To a Saviour who cannot deny.
   Let us tell him in brief,
   That of sinners we're chief,
But we long to be ready to die.

   We've his word and his oath,
   His dear blood seal'd them both,
And we're sure the Almighty can't lie;
   That if we don't delay,
   To believe, watch, and pray,
He will soon make us ready to die.

   Then with sword, staff, and shield,
   Let us enter the field,
And make all our proud enemies fly;
   In the strength of our king
   We shall victory sing,
Till the Lord sees us ready to die.

   When the battle is won,
   And our race fully run,
We to mansions of glory shall fly;
   There eternally praise
   The blest Ancient of Days.
For His love made us ready to die.

SONG L
THE ROYAL GEORGE[95]

No history can parallel
The dreadful tale I mean to tell;
The tidings sent us from on board
Sufficiently can't be deplor'd.

CHORUS

Britons lament, this loss so large,
Kempenfelt, and the Royal George.

It was at Spithead where she lay,
And had on board, that fatal day,
Well nigh a thousand of both sex,
Perhaps two-thirds betwixt the decks.

Britons, &c.

The ship was heel'd for some repair,
With ports not lash'd for want of care,
And lying just athwart the tide,
By which we lost our navy's pride.

What numbers of unthinking souls,
Were doubtless merry o'er their bowls,

---

[95] This song relates to the loss of the above-named vessel at Spithead, on the 29th of August, 1782. The Royal George was the pride of the British navy, and had successfully carried the flags of several of our bravest admirals, including those of Anson, Boscawen, Hawke, Rodney, Lord Howe, and others, none of whom more gallantly upheld our naval supremacy than admiral Kempenfelt. It is supposed that besides the gallant commander seven or eight hundred persons found a watery grave. The fifth verse describes a sloop (the Lark) which was drawn into the vortex caused by the sinking of the Royal George. This song is more patriotic than most of Mather's. All parties could sincerely join the prayer contained in the last verse. Our author clearly saw the connection between peace and commercial prosperity.

When suddenly a squall arose,
The sea pours in and down she goes.

The whirlpool caus'd by her descent
Drew in a sloop, which also went:
Excluding all the boats could save,
Six hundred got a watery grave.

The lamentation heard all round,
And bodies floating that were drown'd,
Exhibited a dreadful scene:
Sure Neptune did it out of spleen.

Who can conceive or comprehend
The loss of our brave naval friend,
Who on the ocean's briny flood
Had done this land essential good.

May providence our foes disarm,
Defend and keep us from all harm,
And bring about a lasting peace,
That trade and commerce may increase.

SONG LI
THE VALENTINE[96]

A letter charge—I've read at large

---

[96] This was called forth by a valentine which reflected on Mather's writings. Of its merits we remain ignorant. It was attributed to Jonathan Moore, the landlord of the "Old Tankard," Westbar-green. After this smutty production Mather might surely cry quits. The "Tankard" was a famous resort for the grinders who worked at the Old Wheel, Green-lane. The line beginning: "The stuff thou puts into thy guts," finely describes Jonathan's abilities as a trencher man. It is said that on one occasion his wife sent him to seek some barm to brew with. After being absent three days his better half found him at the "Cock," in Hollis-croft, waiting for the barm. He had spent all his money, and in addition had set up a long score. The only defence that Jonathan could offer was that the landlady of the "Cock" promised *to give him the barm.*

The stuff which thou'st indited,
And ere at all I read thy scrawl
  I thought we'd been united;
But since I find thou art inclined
  To prejudice thy neighbour,
For thy reward—thou mean blackguard—
  Take this for thy past labour.

Not far from Hull thy great thick skull
  At first had its existence:
The Westbar-green had better been,
  If thou had'st kept thy distance.
Thy valentine, thou ill-bred swine,
  Displays thy wit, I tell thee,
Thou Battys's mule dost ridicule,
  Altho' it does excel thee.

For actions base, thy native place
  Thou did'st at first abandon;
Wrapt up in rags, hung round with gags,
  Thou had'st scarce a shoe to stand on;
But now thou'rt rais'd—fortune be prais'd,
  By these three last elections;
A man of note, that's got a vote,
  Thou art without objections.

Like some fat hog, or listless log,
  Thou lies in bed each morning
Till nine o'clock,—altho' the cock
  To rise doth give thee warning;
Thou says no prayers, but runs down stairs.
  As though something did fright thee,
And down the yard,—like one that's scared,
  For fear thou should'st beshite thee.

Of all the names, I think Muck James[97]
  Would never stand much bidding,

---

[97] James Ibbotson, or as he was commonly called "t'muckman."

Without pretence,—he'd give twopence
  Each morning for thy midden;
At such a heap how he would leap!
  I wish he could but rent thee
The year about, I make no doubt
  But closely he would tent thee.

With idle bread thou'rt daily fed,
  And oft at others' tables,
Thou swelling hog,—thou'rt like the frog
  We find in Æsop's fables;
Like it thou'lt burst, so do thy worst;
  Not all the world can save thee:
Thy friends backbite, eat, drink and shite;
  The worms in short must have thee.

SONG LII
THE COCK-TAIL FEAST[98]

Soon as old Ball got better,
  A merriment there was appointed,
Creditor as well as debtor

---

[98] This song relates the doings of our ancestors at Scotland-street feast, more especially at the Ball," Furnace-hill, (vide song 35.) Street festivals before the introduction of day police were an intolerable nuisance. The sports consisted of races by both bipeds and quadrupeds; climbing up a greasy pole crowned with a hat or a leg of mutton. This furnished aspiring youths with a stimulus for rising in the world, to the great gratification of the spectators. Bull baiting, cock fighting, and other equally moral amusements gratified our ancestors. The sports of the day usually terminated with singing and dancing at the different public houses. They were termed "penny hops," and were quite common sixty years ago. The quadrupeds on this occasion appear to have vied with each other, and thus added to the humours of "Cock-tail." Blind Stephen and other notorieties appear to have been present at these Bacchanalian orgies. Mather's description is not very fastidious, and it is probable that he often gratified those present by singing his own productions. The spirit of old Samuel, the landlord, seems to have been severely ruffled on this occasion.

Both came to be better acquainted;

Numbers of lads there were present,
   From Kimberworth, Brightside, and Masbro'.
Each with a countenance pleasant,
   His true love did cuddle and clasp her:
Stephen turned out with his fiddle,
   Each lad took his lass by the middle,
Went reeling about like a riddle,
   As if they had been enchanted;
Care, the forerunner of sorrow,
   Was kick'd out of doors till to-morrow,
Not one in his spirit wag narrow,
   Then boh! cried Tiger, undaunted,

CHORUS

Hey! cried Tidswell and Tiger,
   See crowds in almost ev'ry station,
Flocking to Cock-tail most eager.
   To celebrate Ball's restoration.

Tiger, connected with Jemmy,
   Conducted Ball out of the stable,
Join'd in the yard by old Sammy,
   Who ale-fled came from the table:
Ball being well prim'd with ginger
   Was fit to jump over the fences;
Neighbours, as well as each stranger,
   All thought they were out of their senses.
Samuel, who hates to be idle,
Took hold of old Ball by the bridle,
Then gave him a kick made him sidle,
   So went four rounds as they wanted;
Right hand and left they did clever,
Made Jem to squint harder than ever,
He promis'd his partner some liver,
   Then boh! cried Tiger undaunted.

Out jump'd the calf elevated.
　The cow broke her rope and ran after,
Shout upon shout it created,
　And fill'd the spectators with laughter;
Tidswell, the cow was so named,
　Because at that fair they bought her,
She ran at Tiger untamed,
　To fork him as nature had taught her.
Tiger at that was displeas'd,
Which caus'd a fresh dust to be rais'd;
Her nose in a moment he seiz'd,
　At which old Samuel ranted.
Tidswell took off like be-madded,
O'er mother and daughter she gadded.
Huzzas in abundance were added,
　Then boh ! cried Tiger undaunted.

Stephen, tho' blind as a beetle,
　Laugh'd hard at Hannah's disaster;
He lost no time with his fiddle,
　His elbow went quicker and faster.
Ball cut such new-fashioned capers,
　Which really by-standers amaz'd;
All his four feet were as tapers,
　The pavement it perfectly blaz'd:
Samuel, nor no one that join'd him,
Durst venture their carcase behind him,
Tho' age in a manner did blind him;
　No colt could win him 'twas granted,
Tidswell caught Tiger and toss'd him,
　Quite out of the ring till she'd lost him,
Tho' many a bruise it did cost him,
　Still boh! cried Tiger undaunted.

Sam el imbib'd a wrong spirit,
　Tho' hundreds and thousands were charm'd,
Curs'd poor old Ball for his merit,
　And Jem who his fundament warm'd:

Tidswell bled hard at her snort-horn,
   Where Tiger was constantly aiming,
That by old Sam'el was not borne,
   And thus he began of exclaiming:
Blow up the gantries and barrels,
   Kate's mouse-trap, that breeder of quarrels,
And all the night owls without laurels,
   By which our stag room is haunted;

Sounding-board, hat, balloon-bonnet,
   That head-dress, my curse be upon it,
For ever this shall be my sonnet,
   Then boh! cried Tiger undaunted.

THE COCK-TAIL FEAST[99]

---

[99] This is a continuation of the festive season, and shows further amusements. The exploits of Tiger and Tidswell would doubtless prove exciting, more especially mother Jenkinson's disaster. There are other celebrities described by their nick names. "Hotbread" was one of the night watchmen, and helped to eke out his subsistence by selling fruit. Many jokes were practised at his expense. For the protection of the watch men in stormy weather the town trustees erected five or six watch boxes in various parts of the town. A party of scissors grinders who had been at a trade meeting at Mr. Hinchcliffe's, the "Greyhound," Gibraltar, looked into the "box" which stood at the bottom of Snig-hill, and found the *guardian* of the night fast asleep. This discovery caused one of them to go back into Spring-street to *borrow* a clothes line which some good woman had left out all night. With this cord they tied "Hotbread "in his box, and forcibly hoisted him on their shoulders. This rough proceeding roused the *vigilance* of Tommy, who began lustily to cry "athithtance!" "athithtance !" "If yo don't lay me *down I'll tak yo up!*" The grinders, heedless of his threats, carried him into the middle of the goit at Mill-sands, and left him there to cool. On another occasion when "Hotbread" was in Mulberry-street vending his fruit, some of the workmen of Messrs. Holy, Wilkinson and Co. called out of the window for some apples, requesting one of the lads, who was in the street, to carry them upstairs. A brazier put the coppers in the fire and threw them out of the window, and poor Tommy found that they were either too *heavy* or too *hot* for him to carry. He felt this to be an insult not to be tolerated by a *public character*, so he went to complain to Mr.

PART SECOND

Oceans to drink being call'd for,
  Hot cuddle-me-buff was the liquor,
"Wife of my own" Jemmy call for,
  Old Hannah cried "Stephen" play quicker.

Off they west after each other,
  As if they had quicksilver in them,
Join'd by first one then another,
  You never saw aught that could win them,
Setting down sides then up again,
Crossing o'er couples, so up again,
Sam'el inspired with his cup again,
  Of his activity vaunted;
Ball being prim'd with the rest of them,
Farted and kick'd with the best of them,
Seemingly made a mere jest of them,
  Boh! cried Tiger undaunted.

CHORUS

Hey! Tidswell and Tiger,
Dame Jenkinson, look to your smock-tail,
Crowds from all quarters ran eager.
  To scamper amongst them in Cock-tail.

Tidswell when Tiger pursuing
  Threw up mother Jenkinson's smock-tail;

Holy. Hotbread, however, was doomed to realise the force of Shakespeare's assertion that "Misfortunes never come single," for he had no sooner reached the landing than he was metamorphosed by receiving a copious shower of whitening and water on his devoted head, Mr. Holy's endeavours to find out the guilty party were unavailing. With one exception all the workmen assured their employer they were innocent. The excepted workman gravely assured him that he had not *seen* the trick performed. This was quite true, because before giving "Hotbread" a whitewashing he *shut his eyes.*

Jem whilst her marigold viewing,
 Cried hey! for the humours in Cock-tail!
One o'er another they tumbled,
 You scarce could see faces for arses;
Tiger at some of them grumbled,
 Supposing some arses were faces.
Some were intent upon heel and toe.
Others ran hedge and bind to and fro,
Sam'el to Ball shouted Stand still, wo!
 Wind a bit lads, for he panted.
Ball thro' some misapprehension,
To Sam'el paid no great attention,
But started at all he could mention;
 Then boh! cried Tiger, undaunted.

Hotbread was there with his barrow.
 So Tiger for mischief ran under;
Tidswell pursued him so narrow,
 Nice apples and pears she did sunder;
Nosey she instantly seated
Betwixt her two horns with her basket;
 Tiger for manners retreated,
And left the old virgin to risk it,
 As she kept gadding thro' thick and thin;
 "Buy or toss, now you are sure to win,
 Up with it, lads, and I'll put it in."
 This was the song that she chaunted—
 "Kill-grief and hearts-ease I've got to sell;
Gingerbread, taste, it will please you well:"
When from her element down she fell,
 Boh! cried Tiger, undaunted.

Ball by a sudden manoeuvre
 His heel turned round to Muck Josey,
Kick'd him thrice over and over,
 With his face at the arse of old Nosey.

Nosey had dropt a face card[100],
   Thro' the fall of her exalted station,
Josey snuffed up very hard,
   Being happy in his situation;
Sam'el at that hung his slipper,
   Whilst Jem with his ginger and pepper
Applied a bit more to Ball's crupper.
   Of which he never repented:
Ball steered his course with fresh vigour,
Determin'd to go to the rigour,
Ran open-mouth'd after bold Tiger,
   Still, Boh! cried Tiger, undaunted.

Tiger run under Ball's belly,
   All danger like Rodney kept scorning,
Some thought he was rather silly,
   For Ball was new frosted that morning;
Sam'el got hurt in the scuffle,
   As Ball his forefeet was advancing,
That seem'd his temper to ruffle,
   And quite put an end to their dancing,
Then they dismis'd in civility,
Talking of Ball's great agility,
Tidswell and Tiger's fidelity,
   Which kind nature implanted;
How the four brutes in particular,
Danc'd with their tails perpendicular,
Straight forwards, sideways, and circular,
   Boh! cried Tiger, undaunted.

SONG LIII
ROUND LEGS[101]

---

[100] 2016 note: OED: to drop a face card (slang) apparently = to defecate. The OED reference is to Mather' song. It is the editor's belief that it as simple as equating royalty (King, Queen, Jack) with turds.)

[101] This song I never saw in print, and therefore cannot vouch for its accuracy. I have carefully collated various versions of it which I have taken

Roundlegs to Wadsley went,
With burying[102] cakes he was sent,
    Fol, lol, lol, la.

Roundlegs tumbled o'er a wall,
Let all his spice cakes fall,
    Fol, lol, lol, la.

Roundlegs turned his mule i'th park,
He then made some nasty wark,
    Fol, lol, lol, la.

Roundlegs next went to the wheel.
To watch them polish steel,
    Fol, lol, lol, la.

Roundlegs was a cunning old toad,
Made three mules carry four-horse load,
    Fol, lol, lol, la.

Roundlegs went to Joel Rose's door,
(He had ne'er been there before,)
    Fol, lol, lol, la.

---

from oral tradition. The tune used to be very popular, and I remember an alderman some years ago creating great laughter in our town council by quoting from this song. For an account of Roundlegs see note to song 19. Mather appears neither to have forgotten nor forgiven those who offended him. There is a playful humour about the song that would be very annoying to the subject of it, especially when sung to a popular tune. In the original edition of Mather's songs the twenty-ninth and the forty-first songs are duplicates. I, therefore, venture to substitute this in the place of one of them: a course which I feel persuaded will not be disapproved by the most ardent admirer of Mather.

[102] Pronounced "berring." It was customary at that time to provide burying cakes, for distribution among the friends of the deceased. George Pearce was a baker, whose cakes were famous. He lived at the bottom of Grindlegate. Roundlegs appears to have been his messenger.

"Does any dead folks live near,
George Pearce has sent me here,"
    Fol, lol, lol, la.

Roundlegs was a famous glutton,
Once he ate a leg of mutton,
    Fol, lol, lol, la.

Roundlegs put a chalk o'er't door,
Then swore he would go there no more,
    Fol, lol, lol, la.

Roundlegs shall be buried i'th fold.
When he's dead and his arse is cold.
    Fol, lol, lol, la.

SONG LIV
THE FACE CARD[103]

From Derbyshire I was transported
  To Rotherham, where I now dwell,

---

[103] The face card is not one of the sweetest subjects, but it illustrates a remarkable freedom of expression among our ancestors. The allusion to the chaise driver in the eighth verse shows that about the principal inns in the old coaching days some of the quaint humour of Sam Weller might have been found. The Angel Inn was kept by Mr. Peach. The Local Register for July 16th, 1793, says "he having been very successful in gathering his harvest treated his mowers, &c., with a plentiful dinner at his farm, at Carbrook, and brought them to his house in coaches drawn by four horses each, with bands of music. The cavalcade proceeded to the Angel, where a cold collation was served to the company, and Mrs. Peach gave half-a-dozen very large bowls of cold posset." The harvest of that year was remarkably early. Mr. Peach was a very spirited coach proprietor. When opposition threatened him in that business he would ran it down. It is said that this spirit was so far carried out that when some opposing coach proprietor carried passengers to London gratuitously, "Old Peach" not only did the same, but gave his passengers a bottle of wine in addition for patronising him.

A fool I was always reported,
   The people of Bakewell can tell;
I hector and talk about fighting,
   Till I am amazingly scar'd;
When scolding I'm ready for sh—g,
When struck, then I drop a face card.

You've heard with what bullocking speeches,
   When absent from home, not in want,
I sold from my arse my new breeches,
   And gave half-a-crown to recant;
The buyer he quickly resign'd them,
   And cast them away from him, yards,
When he saw how well I had lin'd them,
   With flushes of trumps and face cards.

My neighbours all envy my genius,
   Because I endeavour to thrive;
Five pounds I turn'd into five guineas
   By making the cypher a five.
The assignees thought I could conjure,
   Till the bill and the books were compar'd,
But now they incessantly grumble,
   And throw in my teeth the face card.

At Ecclesfield, after receiving
   A free and most generous treat,
Before I could well think of leaving
   My friend I attempted to cheat;
Altho' to his kindness a debtor,
   By gratitude doubly debarr'd,
Yet cleanliness taught me no better
   Than drop in his house a face card.

Then to it we fell with a rattle,
   Broke buffets, stools, tables, and chairs;
But just in the midst of the battle,
   We both tumbled down't cellar stairs.

Strong beer in the barrels was jumbled,
  Here Bacchus and Mars rather jarr'd,
My pride he sufficiently humbled.
  By making me drop a face card.

At Sheffield, inspired by the barrel,
  I let them know Bullocking Dick;
As usual I kick'd up a quarrel
  With one whom I'd play'd a foul trick;
The landlady stept in betwixt us,
  For which she deserved a reward,
Ere she in our seats had refix'd us,
  I privately drop'd a face card.

My wife, a good kind of creature,
  Who knew me a coward in grain,
Says, "Dickey, our good legislators
  On fighters inflicteth much pain,
I pray thee go home with me quickly,
  Thy new leather breeches thou'st marr'd;
I find myself turn very sickly,
  By smelling thou'st drop'd a face card."

Before we got opposite Peach's
  The legs of the knaves were display'd,
From under the hams of my breeches,
  On which a young chaisedriver said—
"Here's Dick made a crack in his manners,
  His new leather breeches he's marr'd,
He has not drop'd all the four honours,
  'Tis nought but a simple face card."

The legs of my Jack's growing longer,
  Some enter'd the tops of my pumps;
The streets with spectators grew stronger,
  Who all shouted out "hearts are trumps!"
The ace, king and queen quickly follow'd,
  Small trumps, I play'd near forty yards;

If all the whole pack I had swallowed,
  I could not have drop'd more face cards.

This wicked chaisedriver turn'd poet,
  And put my misfortunes in print;
In order that people might know it,
  He's giv'n the public this hint;
So now I'm perplex'd above measure,
  By boys and insulting blackguards,
Who cry as I walk out at leisure,
  "That's Dickey that drops the face cards."

A fool you may bray in a mortar,
  And he will remain a fool still;
Poor Dick till his days are cut shorter,
  His new leather breeches will fill;
A wit might as easily manage
  To reconcile fire and dry hards,
And plough up both Mam-Tor and Stanedge,
  As stop him from dropping face cards.

SONG LV
THE RIMSEY OLD MAN[104]

Burton wheel[105] grinders declare upon honour
  That Patty's front room lets for more than a hull;
Not without reason they cry fie upon her,
  And jovial sing thus when their pitcher is full:

---

[104] Mather appears to have been most unscrupulous in his attacks on private character. Whether the person meant in this song was the lascivious man that Mather describes him is now of little consequence. Be that as it may, such songs would be very annoying to the persons lampooned.

[105] Barton wheel. The old Twelve o'clock water-wheel once belonged to the Bartons, of Royds mill, whose pedigree, extending over 400 years, may be found at page 236 of Hunter's "Hallamshire." For the beauties of Claywood, (South-street, Park) see note, page 7, of the before-mentioned history.

I saw John wonderful diligent,
Taking dimensions of Patty's front tenement,
When to the parlour door tip-toe I peeping went,
   At the lascivious rimsey old man.

CHORUS

Man, says one, look into chronology,
Scale the wild mountains of his genealogy,
Asses and goats, without any apology,
Were his forefathers, deny it who can.

John knows adultery's strictly forbidden,
  Yet still he presumes to transgress the command,
As if it could from Omniscience be hidden,
  He acts like a he-goat that can't understand.
    The people all round cry in sincerity,
    He is the vilest of Adam's posterity,
    Treat him, they say, with the utmost severity,
      He's a lascivious rimsey old man.

Joseph retreats, and stands pimp with submission,
  While John runs flaming with lust to his wife;
Patty was always of that disposition,
  She ne'er was content with one man in her life.
    Lust for lust, as it is rendered,
    And when repeatedly they have engendered,
    Patty by Joe is embraced when tendered
      By that lascivious rimsey old man.

John some time since had a tenant a grinder
  Whose wife paid the rent, if the neighbours don't He;
Strict in an article he did bind her,
  To go for acquittance five stories high.
    This she did, looking for recompense,
    And then indicted him, risking the consequence:
    John was the scribe, the devil the evidence,—
      O that lascivious rimsey old man.

Much like a fox by the huntsman's tantivy,
  He's oft been put up when the trees were in leaf,
Hedges and woods to his whoredoms are privy,
  As thus sung the birds in Clay-wood and Burngreave.
     Johnny, whose ways are all iniquity,
     Often goes there with his whores in obscurity,
     Taking no thought in the least of futurity,—
       He's a lascivious rimsey old man.

John I presume has no more felicity
  Than the wild jackass that ranges the moors,
His element is a vast multiplicity
  Of most abandoned adulterous whores.
     Since his choice is their society,
     Daily embracing forbidden variety,
     May we not say with the strictest propriety,
       He is a mischevious rimsey old man ?

SONGS NOT IN 1862 EDITION

THE STANDARD OF FREEDOM

In sweet Liberty's cause I would yield up my life,
For tis bondage that renders it base
I'll soon quit the land of contention and strife,
To find out a happier place,
Where no tyrants or slaves are known to exist,
Nor Whigs or base Tories mislead them,
But each patriot soul may join to the last
To support the great Standard of Freedom.
Then under the shade of my fig-tree enjoy
in sweet solace and talk with my friends
With no taxes to grieve me – nor tithes to destroy
The sweet blessings that Providence sends
I'll keep in reserve Tom Paine's "Rights of Man,"
And lend them to all that can read them;
And tell those that can't 'twas he found the plan

To restore the great Standard of Freedom

In sweet peace and plenty, Love crowns each season
With a partner that's just to my mind,
My religion's not priestcraft, but blest truth and reason, to love God,
and do good to mankind,
And when that old age to life brings a close,
The praises of fools I'll not heed them;
But engrave on my tomb, where my ashes repose,
The remains of a true son of Freedom.

HER MASTER'S BED

When that I lived in Derbyshire,
   One night to Sheffield town I came,
To a young lass that there did dwell,
   But I don't care to tell her name,
Her master and dame being gone from home,
   The time that I went to her,
And very much she made of me,
   For I'd been us'd to woo her.

She gave me meat and scran to eat,
   Till I was well contented,
And since I've been so long from her,
   She sorely me lamented;
We made a tankard of rum punch,
   And when we had made an end on't,
I said we'll lie together this night,
   I'll do thee no harm depend on't.

Then straight up stairs we both did go,
   Into her Master's chamber,
She said if her daddy he should know,
   He'd either kill or lame her,
Ne'er mind thy daddy I replied,
   This night we'll lie together,

Young women are apt to deny a thing,
    When to take it then they'd rather.

O! then I stript and into bed,
    And she laid her down by me,
I said my dear come get into bed,
    Cans't thou find in thy heart to deny me;
She stript all off to her under petty-coat,
    And into bed she ventured,
I impatient was to be at the sport,
    But immediately I entered.

Then her motion she kept so compleat,
    This pleas'd me out of measure,
And since I'd been so long from her,
    O I thank'd her for my pleasure;
So then I lay in her arms all night,
    Till five o'clock next morning,
The Sun shone in the window so bright,
    Then I began of performing.

As thus I lay in her Master's bed,
    With red silk curtains around me,
A pretty lass down by my side,
    No greater joys abound me,
The I cheerfully lift up my voice,
    Said while we are together,
My dear let's have another touch,
    For it's charming pleasant weather.

When I awoke at five o'clock,
    All round the room I gaz'd,
I saw three large looking glasses,
    This almost me amaz'd;
The frames were gilt with gold,
    They were to admiration,
Chairs were cover'd with red velvet,
    This was worth my observation.

But when I awoke at nine o'clock,
  I found small satisfaction,
Of my last night's debauchery,
  And all my wicked actions,
For kissing's an insipid thing,
  Wherever it doth follow,
It only brings men's minds to ease,
  And all their bones to sorrow.

SHEFFIELD THE BLACK

Where slowly down the vale a river runs,
  Of dark complexion like its crooked sons;
In a fair country, stands a filthy town,
  By bugs and butchers held in high renown;
Sheffield the Black – in ugliness supreme;
  Yet ugly Sheffield is my dirty theme.
Ah, luckless he, who in unhappy hour
  Is doomed to walk our streets beneath the shower,
No friendly spout from the projecting paves,
  The copious tribute of the clouds receives,
But headlong from the roof, in sooty showers,
  Prone on the hapless passenger it pours.
While on our moonless evenings, dark and damp,
  Imprudent thrift denies the public lamp
And many a dunghill graces many a street.
  Whole streams of rubbish and whole seas of mud;
With turnip tops, potato peelings join,
  And to their cast garments, peas and beans combine,
Providing pigs and ducks with goodly cheer;
  To pigs and ducks our streets are ever dear,
May no audacious scavenger presume to wield the rake, the shovel or the broom

HEY TURK

One night of late, at ten o'clock, as I was sat reflecting
On the sacks of wheat and bags of flour that I had been collecting,
Toll goes the market bell, just as I was a-thinking
I'd smoke my pipe and merry be, and end the night in drinking.
    Hey, my dog Turk, go thee and lurk!
      He howl'd with joy to hear me;
    For in such awe I have him now,
      That he both loves and fears me.

I'll fetch the lantern and candle out, and search where I suspect 'em,
Amongst the stalls and on the walls for there Turk may detect 'em;
I cried 'Hallo,' you're up there I know, cannot I hear you prating?
I'll lock you up until the morn, for I am tired of waiting.
    Hey, my dog Turk, go thee and lurk!
      For thou art very cunning;
    I'll stop at the gates and break their pates,
      As fast as they come running.

MISCELLANEOUS SONGS FROM THE 1862 EDITION

SATURDAY NIGHT[106]

Ye muses who mount on Parnassian towers,
Come trooping to Sheffield, and help me to sing
The time when our sons have all got out their sours,
And relate all the joys that our Saturdays bring.
    But hard words and Greek-em

---

[106] This song was a great favourite many years ago. I cannot ascertain who was the author; it has been attributed to the person who wrote the song, part of which is quoted in a note, to Ben Eyre (page 17.) For the copy of it, as well as of the next song, I am indebted to Mr. Thos. Rowbotham of the People's College, to whom I am under great obligations. I do not know any person who possesses a greater store of Sheffield lore than my esteemed friend.

    Let learned folks speak-em;
It's epic and tragic, bombastic we'll write;
    And loudly we'll sing O,
    In plain English lingo,
The stirrings in Sheffield on Saturday night.

The barbers their gimcracks in readiness getting,
Their lather-box, looking-glass, shaving cloth clean;
Clean towels, hot water, their razors are whetting,
To mow the ripe harvest that grows on the chin.
    Then into the shop, Sir,
    With long beard you pop, Sir,
And there get your chin painted all over white;
    And one may suppose, Sir,
    Fast hold of your nose, Sir,
They'll fettle your phiz on a Saturday night.

Then see you pop in, Sir; nor doubt or delay, Sir,
And turn Sabbath-breaker and clergistic rule;
Be wise and beware of the Sunday morn razor,
And always avoid the cheap torturing tool.
    With the sweat on your chin, Sir,
    You'll grumble and grin, Sir,
Sure as the dull edge on your front shall alight;
    If you ax him to whet, Sir,
    He'll cry in a pet, Sir,
You should come to be shaved on a Saturday night,

Then maids with their baskets are to and fro walking,
In Shambles to bargain with butchers for meat;
While some ballad singers so slowly are walking,
And warbling so sweetly their lays in the street.
    There's calendars crying,
    And people "come buying"
Around this odd fellow in crowds such a sight;
    For as suits your palates,
    Confessions and ballads,
Are all at your service on Saturday night.

Of hammers and files no more of their din is,
Round the door of the warehouse the workmen are ranged,
While the masters their bank notes and snug little guineas
Are counting and strutting about to get changed.
    Having reckon'd they ne'er stop,
    But joy to the beer-shop,
Where the fumes of tobacco and stingo invite;
    And the oven inhabits
    A store of Welsh rabbits[107]
To feast jovial fellows on Saturday night.

Then while o'er the tankard such fun they are raising,
Full often will fate their enjoyments annoy:
A scolding wife puts her unwelcome face in,
An intruding guest that breaks in on their joy.
    "What! here again, Billy;
    Why sure, man, tha'rt silly;
O'd burn thee, come home, or o'l dit up thy sight."
    "How so, now, my jewel,
    I'm sure that is cruel,
To begrudge one a sup on a Saturday night."

Then while Sheffield liquor around they are pushing
There's many a chorus melodious to rise;
Though oft interrupted by merchants who rush in
With "Cockles alive O!" or "Hot mutton pies!"
    Perhaps you may choose, Sir,
    To pore o'er the news, Sir,
And tell whether matters go wrong or go right;
    For all ranks and conditions
    Commence politicians
While sat at the alehouse on Saturday night.

As through the dark alleys, if slily one pops,
What fun they may hear, if an ear they will lend;

---

[107] Toasted cheese.

Such sighs and soft wishes from lads and from lasses,
Who tell their fond tales at an entry end.
    Then he to his truelove
    Says, "Polly, adieu, love,"
And kisses and squeezes his lassie so tight;
    And softly she'll cry, Sir,
    She'll blush and say, "Fie, Sir,
Can't you stay a bit longer ?—it's Saturday night."

And if a variety here you be craving,
There's butter, there's fruit, there's flesh, and there's fish;
There's buying and selling, and courting and shaving,
And pray, Sir, what else is there that you could wish?
    Thus with drinking and smoking,
    And laughing and joking,
They put wrinkled sorrow and care to the flight;
    And over the stingo
    They laugh, chat, and sing, O!
And merrily welcome each Saturday night.

THE JOVIAL CUTLERS[108]

---

[108] I have often inquired about the author of this song, but have never been able to ascertain who he was. An old cutler told me that he thought old "Bone-heft" wrote it. He was an old cutler who made bone-handled knives 70 or 80 years since, beyond this my informant could not get. The honours of Saint Monday are set forth in this song. The wife reminding her husband about his "sours" is very expressive. The custom of souring work is "more honoured in the breach than the observance." Perhaps we have no account of contentions between husband and wife more graphic than that here recorded: to throw the liquor in his face is an exploit that has often been performed. I once witnessed a scene fit to be described by the pen of a Dickens or the pencil of a Wilkie. A woman came to the public-house to fetch her husband home, and soon gave evidence of the apostle's words, that the "tongue is an unruly member." This quickly roused the indignation of him who had vowed "to love and to cherish" her; instead of doing either, he threatened to thrash her unless she went about her business. This she refused, and with the courage of an Amazon declared that if any one would hold the child she would try which was the "better man." The sanitary state of the baby was such that for a while no

TUNE—*"Cease, rude Boreas"*

Brother workmen, cease your labour,
Lay your files and hammers by;
Listen while a brother neighbour
Sings a cutler's destiny—
How upon a good Saint Monday,
Sitting by the smithy fire,
Telling what's been done o't Sunday,
And in cheerful mirth conspire,
    Soon I hear the trap-door rise up,
    On the ladder stands my wife:
    "Damn thee, Jack, I'll dust thy eyes up,
    Thou leads a plaguy drunken life;
    Here thou sits instead of working,
    Wi'thy pitcher on thy knee;
    Curse thee, thou'd be always lurking,
    And I may slave myself for thee."

Now her passion sets her tongue fast,
Rage won't give her malice sway;
And her clapper, which did ring fast,
For want of breath is forced to stay;
Her eyes boil up with fire and fury,
Anger makes her cheek look pale;
And her power to let the men see,
Again her voice our ears assail:
    "Ah! thou great, fat, idle devil,
    Now I see thy goings on;
    Here thou sits all't day to revel,
    Ne'er a stroke o' wark thou's done;
    If thou canst but get thy tankard

---

one volunteered to take it in charge, but at last a waggish carter told her to put in his smock-frock. This was no sooner said than done: the good woman led off *a la Tom Sayers*, when, but for the interference of others, she would soon have demonstrated that she was indeed the *better* half of her sottish husband.

> Thou neither thinks o'wark nor me:
> Curse thee, I was sorely hampered
> When I married a rogue like thee."

All yon who, blinded by delusion,
Matrimony never know,
Cannot judge of my confusion,
But may think my tale untrue,
For her foul tongue it's past bearing,
Her looks are full of foul disdain;
Ranting, railing, tearing, swearing,
Hark! her clapper rings again.
> "See thee, look what stays I've gotten,
> See thee, what a pair o'shoes;
> Gown and petticoat half rotten,
> Ne'er a whole stitch in my hose,
> Whilst broil'd up with noise and racket,
> Thou'd'st swallow more than would fill a butt—
> Damn it, tak'it—devil, tak'it,
> It's better there than in thy gut."

Now she speaks with motion quicker
Than my boring stick at a Friday's[109] pace;
She throws the generous sparkling liquor
With all her fury in my face;
My eyes, my apron, and my breeches,
My poor shirt sleeves are drench'd with ale.
Something bad my dear bewitches,
Again to vex us with her tale.
> "Pray thee, look here, all the forenoon
> Thou's wasted wi' thy idle way;
> When does t'a mean to get thy sours done?
> Thy mester wants 'em in to-day;
> Thou knows I hate to broil and quarrel,
> But I've neither soap nor tea;
> O'd burn thee, Jack, forsake thy barrel,
> Or never more thou'st lie wi'me."

---

[109] Cutlers work hard on Fridays.

Now once more on joys be thinking,
Since hard scolding's tired my wife;
The course is clear, let's have some drink in,
And toast a jovial cutler's life;
For her foul tongue, Oh! fie upon her,
Shall we our pleasures thus give o'er?
No! we will good Saint Monday honour,
When brawling wives shall be no more.

THE CUTLER'S SONG[110]

So, neibours, how done yo ?—yore sat in a row;
By the mass, man, oh loike to mak one in a show;
Why don't these play-acting foak lake away ?
I'm cum, yo mun know, to hear what theyne to say.
Where are they ? They're goan; if they doant cum agean
I'll uphoud 'em for plaing, for I'll e'en oss mysen;
Varry weel, varry weel, sailor lads, hearts of oak,
    Cutlers' lads, hearts of steel.

You beaus and you bloods, you bucks and you rakes,
You ne'er eat a meal sweet industry makes.
Despise us mechanics! We're tradesmen, 'tis true;
But without us mechanics, what would the world do?
Could trees be clipp'd, sheep be shorn, clothes be cut out,
Without Sheffield shears? No, no, without doubt.
Nor let landed men our black smithies be scorning,
For without scythes and sickles how could folk get corn in?

---

[110] This song was written about 80 years ago, and was sang at the theatre with great applause at the benefit of the author, Alex. Stephens. The verse beginning "The blades they are sent," &c. is very expressive of the grinder's trade. The introduction is not the genuine dialect of Sheffield; the words "lake" and "neibours" for example. This song is set-up from a printed copy belonging to my fellow-workman Mr. Vincent Bradbury, who kindly lent it for the occasion.

The great poet Chaucer has praised Sheffield whittles,
For without knives and forks how could folk eat their victuals?
As for our penknives extensive our trade is,
Likewise our scissors, they're praised by the ladies;
Our razors long time abroad famous have been,
Like our women and wit, they're bright but they're keen.
The bounty of nature on Sheffield town smiles,
Yet could other trades work if we did not make files?

Why don't we supply them, through all Europe we're known,
To the Indies our goods go, through Afric' they're shown;
Likewise throughout the American coast
The cutlers of Sheffield their commerce can boast:
Go where you will, or with what else goods, we'll meet 'em;
They're like our soldiers and sailors, none ever can beat 'em.
But I've spoke long enough about this or that trade,
So I'll sing you a song how a penknife is made.

SONG

Come chorus, my lads, at least favour my verse,
The skill of a cutler I mean to rehearse;
At his stithy he stands black, and all black his clothes,
Yet more black at the bottom are court-pensioned beaux.
To no party a slave, yet his part he'll maintain;
Like his anvil he's steady, to labour his ready;
He drinks, then he works, boys, again and again.

The print he first forms for the bolster of scales,
Yet whilst he is forging he forges no tales;
The scales being finished on the springs he begins,
With hammer in hand, as he works thus he sings—
    To no party, &c.

The blades they are forged—yet look on men's lives,
You'll find there are wasters in more things than knives;
For as health and wealth's wasted and honour is wreck'd,
As some blades they are flaw'd, so some men's skulls are

crack'd.

>   To no party, &c.

We break points, and point them to make them right length,
We harden and temper to fix them in strength;
So our hearts are right harden'd by loyalty's cause,
And we temper our minds by society's laws,

>   To no party, &c,

The blades they are sent to the wheel to be ground,
So we find that the grinding trade goes the world round;
The rich grind the poor, and the great grind the small,
Thus we grind one another till death grinds us all.

>   To no party, &c.

About boring and filing what next shall I sing,
Of sharpening the wire and driving the pin;
Half buff'd and gloss'd, thus we finish away,
Strike the mark, set the edge, wrap them up, and huzza.

>   To no party, &c.

Give me leave, Sheffield friends, with a wish to conclude,
May our orders be great and our markets be good;
And when death wraps us up, and life's order's complete,
A good market in heaven may each Sheffield lad meet.
Strive this wish to fulfil, boys, our friends will say then,
In life we were steady, for death we were ready,
May we live thus and die thus, Amen and Amen.

>   To no party, &c,

THE CUTLIN' HEROES[111]

---

[111] A somewhat different version of this very expressive song appears in the "Sheffield Dialect," I am not aware whether Mr. Abel Bywater obtained the song from oral sources or printed copy. The third verse is not in his copy. The line relating to "flat-backs" and "spotted hefts" is more consistent with the rest of the song than the duplicate lines in the first and fourth verses of the "Shevvild Chap's" version. The "yoller bellies an't nickerpeckers" seems in those days to have been the gods of the gallery at

Cum all yo cutlin heroes, where'ersome'er yo be,
All yo wot works at flat-backs, cum lissen unto me;
      A baskitful for a shillin,
      To mak em we are willin,
For flat-backs and spotted hefts we daily mun be sellin,
Or swap em for red herrins, ahr bellies to be fillin.

A baskitful o'flat-backs o'm shure we'll mak, or mooar,
To ger reit into't gallara, whear we can rant an rooar,
      Throw flat-backs, stooans, an sticks,
      Red herrins, booans an bricks;
If they dooant play Nansa's fansa, or onna tune we fix,
We'll do the best at e'er we can to braik sum o' ther necks.

'T yoller bellies[112] an't nickerpeckers[113] are we us combined,
An when we get i't gallara, my lads, all in a mind;
      An then we stamp away,
      An mak Joe Taylor[114] play
"Nottingham Races" quickly withaht ony mooar delay,
Or else we'll break his fiddlestick.—All in a mind, huzza.

Hey, Jont, lad, is that thee, where are ta waddlin to?
Dusta work at flat-backs yit, as thah's been used to do?
      Hah, cum an tha's gooa wimma,
      An a sample o will gi' tha;
It's won at o've just foorged uppa Jeffra's bran new stidda;
Look at it weel, it duz excell all't flat-backs e ahr smitha.

---

the theatre. For the present version of this song the public will be indebted to Mr. John Eyre, silver plate manufacturer, to whom I am much obliged for the kind manner in which he presented me with the copy. Mr. Eyre says that he took the song from an old copy which he saw a many years ago. It is very probable, therefore, that the present version of the song is the correct one.

[112] Grinders

[113] Filecutters

[114] Joe Taylor, the leader of the band at the theatre.

Let's send for a pitcher o'ale, lad, for o'm gerrin varra droi ,
O'm ommast chooakt we smitha sleek, the wind it is so hoi;
      Ge Rafe an Jer a drop,
      They sen they cannot stop,
They're e sich a moita hurra to get to't penny hop,
An they sware they'll knock em all et heead if they dooant lead off.

Here's Steem at lives at Heela, he'll soon be here, o kno,
He's larnt a new Makkarona step, the best yo ivver saw:
      He has it sooa compleat,
      He troies up ivvera street,
An ommast braiks all't pavors we swattin dahn his feet,
An Anak troies to beat him whenivver they dun meet.

We'll raise a tail be Sunda, Steem; o kno whoa's one to sell;
We'll tee a hammer heead at end, to mak it balance well:
      It's a reit new Lunnon tail;
      We'll ware it kail for kail;
Ahr Anak browt it wi' him, that neit he cum be't mail;
We'll drink success unto it—hey! Jont, lad, teem aht t'ale.

ROTHERHAM FAIR[115]

I wonder, gentlemen, you crave
  A song from such an elf, Sirs,
I've only one about "Rotherham Fair,"
  Which you'll find I made myself, Sirs.

---

[115] I believe that this song was never before printed. Like many productions of a local character, it freely describes the peculiarities of some of the persons introduced. It was written soon after the Battle of Waterloo, and was often sung by the Author, old Jemmy Hinchcliffe, who at the end of each verse accompanied himself on the dram, by beating his Tol der rol lol. The older portion of the community will remember the pig market being in the Wicker, hence the attack on the author's legs.

Spoken.—I went to Mackenzie's *pop shop* to buy a bran new suit of clothes, which cost five shillings all but four and tenpence halfpenny. A fine new hat without brim; a pair of new boots with the tops worn off; my wife, being a hard-working, industrious lass, knitted me a pair of green stockings upon two stack broaches. As I went down the Wicker, past Billy Willey's, I let on some Irish pigs; they thought my legs were cabbage stalks, and I was forced to dash off with my

Tol der rol lol.

Away we went down Brightside lane,
   Mule Harry's cart soon catched us;
It was full of Attercliffe lasses,
   By gad they fully matched us.
Joe Scaife's crook'd legs were like Will Pegs,
   Bob Parker's nose was hooked,
Billy Sweep[116] and me could never agree
   Because our legs were crooked.

As soon as we to Rotherham got,
   I jumped into a squabble,
By joining the company in a song,
   I was soon amongst the rabble,
Who picked my pocket of all my brass,
   Seven Sheffield penny pieces,
Hobson's, Roscoe, Workhouse, Phoenix, Younge's,
      and Leeds's,
   And a weaving devil from Barnsley.
        With his Tol der rol lol.

Spoken.—This loss made us engage with the butchers to drive all their sheep to Sheffield. We made a toll bar of our legs, Billy Sweep

---

[116] "Billy Sampson, the Sweep," was well known in the town long before we had a Ramoneur Association in Sheffield. A friend of mine says, some persons at a public house once filled his hat with treacle and put it on his head, and that it was quite a sight to see Billy lick the sweet streamlets as they coursed down his sooty face.

in the middle, Joe Scaife and I at the sides, when, heigh up! they took Billy's legs for a gate, and in running through they capsized him, *all* of them going one way, while *some* went another; there were only three, and these went off with a
>Tol der rol lol.

I wanted next something to eat,
   Long time my guts had grumbled;
Some ruffians soon began to fight,
   And a baker's stall they tumbled.
I was not an oaf, so I fingered a loaf,
   And popped it under my coat, Sirs,
But "Magnet Jack" had such a gorge,
   He popped it down his throat, Sirs.

Spoken.—The doctors had just turned him out of the Infirmary, incurable, because they could not widen his mouth without shifting his ears. And this made him go about singing

>Tol der rol lol.

Then we thought it was high time
   From Rotherham to depart, Sirs;
Joe Scaife and I did yoke t'oud mare,
   And put her in quite smart, Sirs;
Then rode away without delay,
   With the wenches in the cart, Sirs.
Sung "Tommy Linn," made such a din,
   Which caused t'owd mare to start, Sirs.

Spoken.—She took "boggard," fell o'er a straw, and cut her throat at the *back of her neck*, against a pound of butter; Betty said she was killed, Jack declared he could not speak, Sam had broken three ribs in the calf of his legs, Sukey was down, Rachel on the floor, and Kitty was all daubed with her
>Tol der rol lol.

As soon as I got home at night,

> I bolted into the pantry,
> And there I ate with all my might,
> Until I had cleared the gantry.
> Should I go again I tell you plain,
> No money will I take, Sirs;
> And Betty, good lack! says the next time she'll tak
> A privy upon her back, Sirs.

Spoken.—She'll do this that she may not daub her new gown. I wonder little Boney did not take one to Waterloo, when he dashed off with his breeches full of

> Tol der rol lol.

THE MAYOR OF DONCHESTER[117]:

[117] This satirical production first appeared in the Sheffield Register of February 21st, 1794, with the title as given above, and contained 136 lines. Its next appearance was in 1798 amongst the tales and speculations of "Gabriel Silvertongue" as the poetical production of "Jonathan Starlight." The author had revised and extended the piece by adding about 60 lines. These additions I have enclosed within brackets, the whole being reprinted from the "Whisperer." In 1860 an incomplete version of the original appeared in "Ingledew's Yorkshire Ballads," the lines in italics being entirely omitted. They contain a fine description of corporation feasting. The history of the piece, as it was related to me by my friend the late Alfred Smith, was as follows: In 1793 the mayor and corporation of Doncaster displayed their loyalty by subscribing fifty guineas to purchase flannels, stockings, and other articles to add to the comfort of our troops serving in Flanders. This loyalty was distasteful to the Jacobins of Sheffield, who throughout were opposed to the war. It was proposed by a waggish tanner at Upperthorpe to "hoax" the Mayor (George Pearson, Esq.) This idea was carried out by some of the ardent politicians who frequented "Billy Hill's parlour" to settle the affairs of the nation. The thing tickled the fancy of the youthful poet Montgomery, who put the subject in rhyme to the great amusement of his friends, but sorely to the annoyance of his worship. In the first volume of "Montgomery's Memoirs," page 205, it is stated in a note that "The civic functionary to whom these lines were supposed to apply happening to be in the court (at Doncaster sessions), when the jury had retired to consider their verdict (on Montgomery), said, 'If I were one

A TRUE AND LAMENTABLE TALE

Shewing how his Worship was dubbed a knight a day too soon, and undubbed a day too late, not to be laughed at.

BY PAUL POSITIVE ESQ.
LAUREATE TO THE ASSOCIATION AGAINST REPUBLICANS AND
LEVELLERS

Sweet girls of Pindus, hither bring
  Your drums and bagpipes hollow;
The Mayor of Donchester I sing,
  Assist me, O Apollo!

His Worship is a jolly squire,
And loyal as a spaniel dog;
His zeal as ardent as his kitchen fire;
His head as learned and as big
As that grave philosophic log,
Whereon Puff trims his Worship's Sunday wig;
Nature has ta'en Herculean pains
To scour its ample chambers clean from brains;
And truly at a vast expense
Has purified them quite from wit and sense:
Brains, sense, and wit are such vile vulgar wares
As seldom do disgrace the skulls of mayors.
What of this Mayor of Donchester, I pray?
Sir, he received a letter t'other day.

  Judge, reader, judge what huge surprise,

---

of them I should pronounce him guilty without so much loss of time.' " I have little doubt of the accuracy of Mr. Smith's account, because his memory was very tenacious, and since his death I have verified many things which I wrote from his dictation. The early writings of the poet Mr. Smith would repeat for hours to the gratification of his friends. An intimate friendship existed between Montgomery and Mr. Smith's father, who was one of the persons who gave bail for the youthful bard. The playful humour and keen satire displayed in this piece Montgomery never in after life surpassed. Whether the wag who broke the spell was in the secret or not I am not aware.

Stretch'd like a pair of moons his eyes;
Judge how he gaped for joy, for breath,
And show'd the ruins of his teeth;
Judge how his head sublimer grew;
Judge how his shoulders broaden'd too;
Judge how he threw his arms about;
Judge how he moved his legs so stout;
So big he looked, you would have swore
A giant stood where stood a dwarf before!

[His tender wife beheld his sudden change,
And thought 'twas strange—'twas mortal strange:
"O my sweet stars! Lord! Harry, what's the matter?"
Cried his pale spouse.

"Hark! woman, hold your clatter;
I am a knight, by God!—look there —look there;
A knight! knight I knight! my jewel!" roared the gallant Mayor.
She with a most delicious smile,
Stole the said letter from his Worship's hand:

She read— she trembled all the while,
For verily the lady scarce could stand:
Her hands like admiration stops she raised,
And stood amazed— amazed—amazed!
"Hey, Harry, hey! shall I lady be?"
"A lady, lass? ay, 'faith, a queen!" quoth he.
Thus as he spake, upon her apron's lap
Her hands came dashing down with such a slap,
That made her frightened husband jump,
And tumble retrograde upon his rump;
He fell with such a hollow groan of thunder,
As if a double bass had burst asunder;
She, screaming like a fiddle out of tune,
To 'scape his vengeance—popp'd into a swoon.

There, reader, let the loving turtles lie,
Thou'lt see a resurrection by and bye;]

Meanwhile behold the wonderful epistle,
And if thou canst not laugh—go whistle.

"King George's compliments to Mr. Mayor,
Queen Charlotte also greets his lady fair;
Their gracious Majesties have learned, with pleasure,
How you have sacrificed both time and treasure
On flannel jackets, breeches, stockings, socks,
Also on good warm petticoats and smocks,
To clothe our gallant troops abroad in Flanders,
Their pretty lasses and their smart commanders;
The Queen and Princesses are quite delighted,
And King George swears such deeds shall be requited;
Come, come to London, Sir— come and be knighted."

This note, signed Granville, came by post,
And—cheap enough—a silver sixpence cost.

[Lo ! risen from the hard unfeeling floor,
With aching hearts and bones a little sore,
The wry-faced lady and the limping Mayor
Did for their journey instantly prepare:
The pavement rattles—hark! a chaise and four
Waits their high pleasure at the pompous door.

Just stepping in—my Lady pull'd his sleeve:
"Stop, stop, *Sir* Harry! if we go to London
On this grand *garter*-business we're undone,
Unless you ask the *Corporation's* leave!"

"Alack," he cried "Alack!"
And thumped his wig and staggered back:
His purple nose turned pale with sorrow;
Down dropped his eye and nether lip,
And his hand he placed on either hip;
And dismally exclaimed "Boy, bring the chaise tomorrow."]

No time must now be lost; he goes, he sends

To all his wealthy corporation friends:
The sleek-skined brotherhood soon flocked together,
All in full spirits and full feather;
With double chins and rosy faces,
Pictures of Bacchanalian graces!
[Sepulchral throats, tremendous bellies.
The tombs of flesh, fish, puddings, pies, and jellies!
In solemn state they took their places,
All stared with devouring eyes.]
   Expecting to behold a feast
   Of turtle, exquisitely drest,
And hosts of turkeys, capons, geese, and giblet-pies!
They licked their lips and stroked their maws,
And blest the man that first invented jaws!
Jaws formed so wonderful and so complete;
Jaws that can swear, and pray, and lie and eat.

   When, lo! ah, disappointed paunches;
   Instead of vast sirloins and venison haunches,
   Bright dishes, shining knives and forks,
   Gay bottles, smiling glasses, smacking corks;
   Up rose the Mayor, with grave demeanour,
   And—read the letter—for a dinner!

He ended; and a broad prodigious grin
Screwed every face and tucked up every chin;
But yet mysterious silence hung
A padlock on every tongue.

Till rearing his triumphant crest,
While stars and garters capered in his breast.
Thus the big Mayor the Aldermen addressed:
   "Ha, honest gemmen, don't ye see,
   The King's most gracious Majesty
   Has tumbled quite in love with me?
   Marry! I'll tell ye, worthy gemmen,
   I never knew myself before:
   I've always been a simple yeoman,

Not over rich nor over poor;
To-day a *man*, like one of you,
A *knight* to-morrow I shall ride
In coach and six, with riband blue,
And sword-knot flaming by my side.
On honour's ladder I intend to rise,
Step after step until I touch the skies:
A viscount, earl, a marquis, duke I'll be;
God only knows what may become of me!
And really, gemmen, 'twould be no new thing,
But, in *my turn*—I may—I may be king!"

The Aldermen now started from their places,
And opened all the windows of their faces;
Each viewed the letter with a heart-heaved groan,
And wished with all his might it were his own.
Thus bowing humbly to the *royal* Mayor,
Each offered up a modest prayer.

"Make me," said one, "most gracious Sir!
A learned Lord High Chancellor!"
"Give me," another cried. "the Treasury keys,
And I'll be anything you please!"
"And I," exclaimed a man of weight,
I'll be your Minister of State!"
"Make me your Majesty's physician!';
Cried a poor, lean, consumptive thing;
"But I," quoth one in prime condition,
"Will roast, fry, cook, and cater for the king!"
[Each Alderman asserts pretensions
To places, sinecures, and pensions;
And one and all declared their wishes
To share the Monarch's loaves and fishes.
He, swelling to the size of Atlas big,
Shook a white shower of powder from his wig:
Sublime he strode around the hall,
Majestic towering o'er them all;
   And looked as gracious as you please.

With such a gait, and such a mien,
An old gray gander have I seen,
Stalking across the village green
   Before a flock of geese!]

"Ask, ask," he cried, "whate'er you want,
And all, ay, more than all, I have I'll grant:
Should heaven bestow the golden fleece,
By Jove, I'll make you dukes apiece!

"Fools, fools apiece!" exclaimed a fat
Old wag, who in a comer sat.
"Fools?" cried the Mayor, enraged, confounded:
"Fools?" roared the Aldermen astounded.
"Yes, fools apiece! fools altogether!"
Replied the wicked, sneering wag:
"Fools! Fools!" he cried, "fools of a feather!
I'll let the cat out of the bag:
This letter, Sirs, was never wrote by Grenville,
But forged, I ween, on quite another anvil;
'Tis neither franked, nor does the seal display
A coat of arms magnificent and gay;
Some Jacobin has coined this fabrication,
Just to *befool* our learned Corporation!"

'He spake and smiled—then turned about,
Took down his *chapeau* and went out.
Ghastly and wild his Worship staggered,
And looked as if he had been daggered:
Stung to the stomach with vexation,
The Aldermen all roared "Damnation!"
The meeting, silent as the breaking day,
And soft as mountain snow, dissolved away!

At first his Worship stamped, and stormed, and swore
He never had been made a fool before,
   And therefore could not overlook it;
But second thoughts are best;—his Worship then

Swore he would never be a fool again;
  So put his vengeance in his pocket!

THE VOLUNTEER[118]
PART FIRST

Philosophers say between human and brute
There's a diff'rence too glaring for man to dispute;
An instance which I on experience will found
Will make this hypothesis fall to the ground.

A maltster—reputed for merit and fame,
Has a son who imperfectly nature did frame;
I ne'er with mankind such a monster can class,
For his senses are grosser than those of an ass.

Yet his chaotic brain was possessed with fire,
Which loudly dictated that he should aspire;
So as he the Church and the King did revere.
He without hesitation commenced Volunteer.

The first time he went with his musket to drill
He swore ev'ry man that opposed him he'd kill;

---

[118] This and the two following songs are taken from a small volume printed in Sheffield in 1797. The songs as a whole indicate very freely the religious and political opinions of the author. It is evident from this piece that the volunteers were not popular with the "advanced reformers." At the present day we can scarcely appreciate the annoyance such pieces as the "Volunteer" would give the person thus held up to ridicule. The curious who desire to know the hero may consult "Robinson's Directory" (1797.) Sheffield contained only three maltsters then. I was indebted to the memory of Mr. Alfred Smith for a number of pieces from this work. He was the only person I could find who knew anything about the songs or their author. By subsequent inquiries I found a copy of the work in the possession of Mr. Townsend, to whose kindness I am indebted for the loan of the work, which has enabled me to collate my manuscript with the original. There is neither the printer's name nor the author's. I believe they were the youthful attempts of Charles Sylvester.

Ev'ry dog that he met he presumed to engage,
And thousands of flies fell a prey to his rage.

When more than three months they'd this numbskull been drilling,
He handled his piece as a cow would a shilling;
The commander exclaim'd "What the hell must be done?
Such a blockhead I think ne'er supported a gun,"

By mistaking carcase for brains it is plain,
A series of time must be lavish'd in vain;
In order to know his left hand from his right,
He determin'd performing in private each night.

The family being by Somnus inspired,
He privately into the kitchen retired;
By searching minutely each part of the room,
To his great satisfaction he met with a broom.

After having sometime play'd the part of a fool,
To show how he'd do by a Jacobin's skull,
The head of the broom on the shelf did descend,
And here did his nocturnal exercise end.

The shelf full of pots tumbled down with a thunder,
Which waken'd the fam'ly bewilder'd with wonder;
Who should enter the room but the old man himself,
And he found his brave son laid as flat as the shelf.

Next day came three fellows to fetch him to drill,
Who sought high and low in the malt-house for Will;
At length the old man pronounced loudly, "I think
He's got under the sacks, it is plain, from the stink."

Then each man approach'd, stopping closely his nose,
For they found he'd made terrible work with his clothes
As they could not convey him to drill on their hacks,
He in this situation was left in the sacks.

PART SECOND

Bill's pitiful breeches and shirt
   From the nastiness just separated
The malt-house being clean'd from the dirt,
   And the noxious fumes extricated;
He, to his sad mortification,
Found rapidly in circulation
A scurrilous publication.
   Which things very galling asserted:
Yet as it was lit'rally stated,
He own'd that he evacuated,
   As well as the pot-shelf inverted.

As soon as this wicked production
   Was brought to the house for inspection,
They vow'd on the ballad destruction,
   Though struck with the deepest dejection;
Bill, in a trembling condition,
Took near to the clock his position;
And Jenny, inflamed with ambition,
   Seem'd terribly exasperated;
Old Margery the business hearing,
Was ranting, blaspheming, and swearing,
While Tommy, alas! was appearing
As from the grave emigrated.

The choleric- tempered old fellow,
   Who saw from the bar the confusion,
Did stamp and tremendously bellow,
   Which caused a most horrid conclusion;
The glasses he put into motion
Like so many wrecks on the ocean,
Indeed a six-pounder's explosion
   Could not have spread more consternation;
The neighbours from all quarters flocking,
Did feel such a terrible rocking;
They vowed it was amazingly shocking,
   And look'd for no less than damnation.

Old-slut[119] seeing the family fermented,
   Began to be much disaffected;
Her horns being crooked prevented
   Disasters that might be expected.
   Jewel[120], the fav'rite of Billy,
Though lazy, decrepid, and silly,
Did kick like a two-year-old filly,
   On seeing each long haggard feature;
Bill, as has been represented,
Was so in his belly tormented,
He but with hard squeezing prevented
   A second great effort of nature.

THE QUACK DOCTOR
A COMIC SONG

Would you know who I am, Sir? My name's Dr. Vitum,
The extent of my knowledge is *ad infinitum*;
When old Esculapius dissolved into clay,
I was form'd from his essence called fal de ral de ra.

Here's my tinctura vita?, so famous and clever,
If properly took 'twould make men live for ever;
Why are they such fools as to throw life away
When they all might be saved by my fal de ral de ra?

Your fluids 'twill make overflow like the Nile,
And your guts might be well heard to grumble a mile;
Yea, 'twould gripe you so sore, I'll be bound you would say,
O curse the old Quack and his fal de ral de ra!
Here's my pectoral balsam, distill'd from the sun,[121]

---

[119] The cow.

[120] A favourite old mare.

[121] This is a genuine description of quackery. At a subsequent period of life the author was known for his scientific pursuits. When he visited Sheffield he frequently amused some of the medical profession by singing this song,

And a tincture got pure from the horns of the moon;
With purges and blisters, to scour you away,
And twenty things more for your fal de ral de ra.

My wormcakes with noble success have been tried,
For they ne'er fail to kill when they've e'er been applied;
The patient and worms are both killed in one day,
By one single dose of my fal de ral de ra.

The rich I make pay well for every recipe,
For their pockets as well as their bowels I gripe;
Should a patient be poor, then to take him away,
I give a large dose of my fal de ral de ra.

At curing by killing I so far excel,
That some even deem me an agent from hell;
The soldier abroad cannot sweep more away
Than I with my genuine fal de ral de ra,

A SONG[122]

ADAPTED IN THE YORKSHIRE DIALECT

[The personal pronoun I must be sounded like the French á or aw.]

O Lord haw I love
Yond sweet lass o' the grove,
Tho! shoo's slighted me I cannot hate her!
God help me, think I,
For a year I could cry,
If I lost sitch a good-lookin crater.
Her skin, I can sware,

---

no one enjoying it more heartily than Hall Overend, Esq., whose guest Mr. Sylvester was.

[122] This song I would commend to philologers, The words "napper," "buffin," and "humdrummin," though in use in Sheffield, are not in Hunter's "Glossary," or the Appendix to that work.

Is oz white on oz fair
Az the face ov a new scawer'd trencher;
But zounds if yo try her,
Shoo's sooine so o'fire,
That yo hardly ever can quench her.

One neet be mooine-shine,
I set awt rare on fine,
Yet I thowt if eh saw her twor a wonder;
Lord! whooa shud be there,
Throng a huddlin my dear,
But that thick-heeaded novis Bill Blunder!

Neaw wor not that provooakin,
Withawt onny jooakin,
O! meh tung it went like a bell clapper;
He cursed on he swoar,
If he came onny mooar,
He'd mooast sartinly feel for meh napper.

Then I sed meh dear jewil,
Why ar'ta sooa crewil,
We shud mak a mooast excellent pair;
I've viewed thee all ore,
Booath behint an befooar,
Tha'rt oz like meh oz e'er ta can stare.

'Twor but last Sheveld fair
When we met, I declare,
We put up at the sign o' the Crawn;
Thaw loved me, thaw sed,
An a promise I made,
To buy thee a new woolsey geawn.
Thaw knaws but last year
Nooa man I did fear,
I wor fit for booath cooartin and buflin;
Neaw meh beawty's all gooan,
An I'm all skin an booan,

An meh face iz oz white oz a muffin.

　But that iz not all,
　For meh legs are grown smole,
As the shank ov a sheep, I'll ingage;
　Meh heart it keeps akein,
　Just az iv it wer breykin,
An my ribs ar just like an oud cage.

　Then I sed, cum away,
　For no longer tha'st stay
Wi' sitch-an-a humdrummin chap;
　He when I wer bawn
　To tak howd on her geawn,
Fetch'd my cheek a mooast confaunded slap.

　Od burn it, sed I,
　As tha'rt seemin sooa shy,
I'm determin'd to seek for another;
　An befooar I will be
　Plagued az I've been wi' thee,
I'll hae one az howd az meh muther.

MR. BOURNE AND HIS WIFE[123]

Mr. Bourne and his wife
At breakfast had a strife;
He wanted bread and butter to his tea, fal de ral,

---

[123] This song illustrates a domestic quarrel about a trivial circumstance between a shopkeeper and his wife. I am not aware who wrote it. Mr. William Bourne, the hero of the song, was a hairdresser and perfumer, and resided in Angel-street. The champion on behalf of the lady was supposed to he Mr. Joseph Moore, currier, Snig-hill. The man of leather only proved how foolish it is to meddle with the affairs of other people. There is strong contrast between this domestic quarrel and the fight be
　　tween Nell and Jos (song 7.) This would no doubt be owing to Mr. and Mrs. Bourne being what is vulgarity called *respectable*.

Says she, "I'll rule the roast,
And have a plate of toast,"
So to loggerheads with him went she, fal de ral.

There was one Mr. Moore,
Who lived on the first floor,
A man very strong in the wrist, fal de ral.
He hearing all this clatter
About toast and bread and butter,
Soon knocked down Mr. Bourne with his fist, fal de ral.

Says Mr. Moore, "Ods my life,
You shall not beat your wife,
For it is both a sin and a disgrace," fal de ral.
"Why, then," said Mrs. Bourne,
"That's no business of yourn,"
And she dashed a cup of tea in his face, fal de ral.

"Oh then," said Mr. Moore,
As he sneaked out of the door,
"I surely am a man without brains, fal de ral;
For when married folks are flouting,
If a stranger pops his snout in,
He is sure to get a clouting for his pains," fal de ral.

TOM TOPSAIL[124]

Tom Topsail he died, and the folks piped their eye,
And told of his virtues with many a sigh;
And said when alive he their wants would relieve,
And e'en with a tear his last penny would give;
But when sorely pressed with adversity's gale,

---

[124] This naval song for pathos would not disgrace Dibdin. The authorship is attributed to John Knott. It is a pity that any man capable of writing such songs as this should die a pauper. "The Local Register" of December 2nd, 1840, says, "Decease, in the Workhouse, of John Knott, author of 'Tom Topsail,' 'Ben Block,' " &c.

No soul lent a hand to mend Tom's tatter'd sail;
He through life's last voyage rough storms did endure,
And found none to help him because he was poor.

If a wretch in distress e'er to Tom was made known,
He measured his heart by the worth of his own;
His blubbering eye scarce from tears could refrain,
He felt all his woe, and relieved all his pain!
But when sorely pressed by adversity's gale,
No soul lent a hand to mend Tom's tatter'd sail;
He through life's last voyage rough storms did endure,
And found none to help him because he was poor.

Poor Tom would sometimes at ingratitude sigh,
When those he relieved passed carelessly by;
Yet e'en from his soul he would pity the elves
Who study the interest of none but themselves;
For a goodnatured action, cries Tom, must prevail
With the pilot *above* who can manage the gale:
He through life's last voyage rough storms did endure.
And found none to help him because he was poor,

A friend came at last who had heard of Tom's fate,
He approach'd his straw pallet, but ah! 'twas too late;
The right hand of friendship he warmly applied,
The proffer'd donation Tom calmly denied:
" 'Tis over," he cried, "the bright moment is past,
This old leaky hulk is now sinking at last:
Should the Master approve when the voyage is o'er,
I soon shall be *rich*, although I die *poor*."

THE TRIP MATCH[125]

Both in times ancient and modern we read
Of heroes who have led men to glory;
That battles have been gained both on land and at sea,
Which give pleasure when recorded in story;
Then why can't we praise an old friend and a brother,
Whose innocent pastime never left a stain;
For Bancroft's the lad, there was ne'er such another,
He can beat the whole kingdom again and again.

In good nature and fun few can him excel,
With swagger and bragging he is not hampered;
But courage he will show whenever there's need,
For that's the proper time when it's wanted;
Long time he's been waiting, and none could him withstand,
Till they judged he had failed with old age,
When a challenge from Sheffield he then did receive
From a man that could beat him again and again.

For full fourteen long years have now passed and gone,
Since he showed them how far they were wanting;
His head (like old Time's) is now silvered o'er,
Yet neither age nor gray hairs e'er could daunt him;
They declared he was *old*, and he'd better not try,
But he quickly answered them briefly and plain,

---

[125] These lines celebrate the victory at knur and spell, obtained by Bancroft, of Stannington, over Winterbottom, of Sheffield, on the Doncaster race course, about 40 years ago. I believe the match was for £100 and the championship. If the verses have not the merit of poetic excellence, they show an ardent love of athletic exercises and out-door amusements, so very desirable in manufacturing communities. They were written by Enoch Ratcliff. To realize the force of such songs as this, it is necessary to hear them sung with the accessories of the chorus, which will be heartily joined in by some of the old worthies of Stannington, Loxley, or Upper Hallam. My old friend Jemmy Queen, say the Stannington people, engaged a band to play the "Conquering Hero" before Bancroft who was hoisted on the shoulders of his friends, and carried from the race course to his hotel, on which occasion Jemmy played his tambourine.

You will find me *too old* for my man at the time—
I shall beat your fine Winter again and again.

The match soon was made, and the betting ran high,
And Doncaster race course was shortly agreed on,
Where these two brave heroes their valour might try,
For neither of them before had been beaten;
When the spells were fixed, and they'd taken their ground,
Bancroft then smiling, "What odds," he exclaimed,
"Before three hours' end all the money's our own,
I shall beat their fine Winter again and again,"

When the course was cleared what a sight for the eyes,
For many hundreds of pounds were depending
On which of these heroes would win the first rise;
The great odds upon Winter kept extending;
Bancroft took the lead, and "Look over!" was the cry,
And the Sheffielders swore loudly (I'll maintain),
"We have took him *too soon*, he is not *yet* too old;
He will beat our fine Winter again and again."

Bancroft, like a hero, the game did pursue,
Poor Winter was thus forced to follow;
He ne'er took the lead, boys, all the match through,
But quickly found he was beaten quite hollow;
So now the match is over, and their champion is beat,
All their bragging and swaggering is in vain;
They may choose another, and we'll match our brother;
He can beat the whole kingdom again and again.

THE GRINDERS' HARDSHIPS[126]

---

[126] This song has never before been printed. The author of it is unknown; but as a "fellow feeling makes us wondrous kind," I can sympathize with the "poor grinders." It is probable the song was written by some of the first members of the "Grinders' Misfortune Society," established at Crookes, August 20th, 1804. The present secretary (Mr. Jonathan Wragg) informs me that many years ago the song used to be sung at their annual festivals, the members heartily joining in chorus. I am obliged to him for

It happened in the year eighteen hundred and five,
From May-day to Christmas the season was quite dry,
That all our oldest grinders such a time never knew,
For there's few who brave the hardships that we poor grinders do.
         For there's few, &c.

In summer time we can't work till water does appear,
And if this does not happen the season is severe:
Then our fingers are numb'd by keen winter frosts or snow,
And few can brave the hardships that we poor grinders do.
         For there's few, &c.

When war is proclaimed our masters quickly cry,
"Orders countermanded," our goods we all lay by;
Your prices we must *sattle*, and you'll be *stinted* too—
There's few suffer such hardships as we poor grinders do.
         For there's few, &c.

There seldom comes a clay but our dairy-maid[127] goes wrong.
And if that does not happen, perhaps we break a stone,
Which may wound us for life or give us our final blow,
For there's few that brave such hardships as we poor grinders do.
         For there's few, &c.

There's many a poor grinder who's thus been snatched away
Without a moment's warning to meet the Judgment day;
Before his Judge he *must* appear, his final doom to know—
There are few who brave such hardships as we poor grinders do.
         For there's few, &c.

Thus many a poor grinder, whose family is large,
That with his best endeavours cannot his debts discharge,
When children cry for bread, how pitiful the view,

---

the song as well as a copy of the society's rules. It is very creditable to the grinders (who have always been considered a reckless body of men) to have supported a society for the relief of their misfortunes; and that, after nearly 60 years' experience, it enjoys all the vigour of its youth.

[127] The waterwheel.

Though few can brave such hardships as we poor grinders do.
> For there's few, &c.

So now I must conclude these few humble rhymes
With "Success to all grinders" who suffer in hard times;
I wish them better fortune—their families the same,
And may we never experience such hardships again.
By being further *stinted* and *paying discount too*,
There are few who brave such hardships as we grinders do.
> For there's few, &c.

DR. SHINAR'S THE LAD FOR THE LADIES[128]

Believe me, believe me, in country or town,
No cosmetic trade like mine will go down;
Both young ones and old ones flock at my call,
For wrinkles and pimples I purchase them all;
On that lady's face (bless her heart), I espy
Some freckles (which I'll remove) beneath the left eye;
I change faces pale and wan to the hues of the rose,
And plant on their cheeks what I steal below their nose[129].
  With gumming and rumming I cure blue noses,
  Above all commendation my trade is;
  Smiling Fanny's lovely cheeks (they blush like roses),
  Which plainly show the lasses go
  The nearest way, in this our day,
  To Shinar, the lad for the ladies, O.

Spoken.—Now I'll tell you where I have been, and the wonders I have seen, and show testimonials from the ladies of the following places —Ilchester, Dorchester, Rochester, Winchester, Manchester, Colchester, Woolwich, Dulwich, Highgate, Reigate, Brighton,

---

[128] This song displays the foolishness of quackery. It has never before been printed. It would require a good memory in the author (Jemmy Hinchcliffe) to remember his travels, because nearly, without exception, the places named are realities strung together with a rude rhythm.
[129] Kisses

Leighton, Aughton, Laughton, Buckingham, Rockingham,
Eckington, Beckington, Brompton, Rompton, Hampton, Rampton,
Ransfield, Mansfield, Ecclesfield, Macclesfield, Ilkstone, Silkstone,
Holmesfield, Dronfield, Highergreen, Shiregreen, Caxton, Laxton,
Botley, Totley, Horton, Norton, Beeley, Heeley, and Sheffield.

Once in my coach and four I rattled off to Daventry,
Thence very soon "I was marched off to Coventry;"
(Now this bit of vanity I beg you will pardon);
But I made the ladies smile in fair Covent Garden.
My fine "Mountain Cream" (distilled from the dew),
All the smiles of their youth it did quite renew;
My "Essence of Heartsease" will develop your blushes,
Try my "Pectoral Drops," and you'll warble like thrushes.
  With my gumming and rumming I'll charm your faces,
  That in your lovers' eyes you'll outshine the graces:
  I could you amuse by telling all the news;
  But Mary's eyes tell that I have made her a *belle*.
  And this will show that the lasses go
  The nearest way, in this our day,
  To Shinar, the lad for the ladies, O.

Spoken.—Now listen where I've been, and the marvels I have seen, and been praised in the following places:—Brummagem, Rummagem, Retford, Barking, Deptford, Darking, Worcester, Chester, Glo'ster, Leicester, Rocklington, Pocklington, Dulverton, Wolverton, Oxford, Tuxford, Shrewsbury, Dewsbury, Congleton, Pendleton, Harborough, Scarborough, Eccles, Beccles, Hingham, Bingham, Northumberland, Cumberland, Fairfield, Darfield, Bedale, Edale, Gainsborough, Stainsborough, Ferrybridge, Boroughbridge, Rotherham, Botherham, Handsworth, Wandsworth, Attercliffe, and Sheffield.

And these things show all the lasses go
In this our day, and truly pray
For Shinar, the lad for the ladies, O.

PRISON AMUSEMENTS
VERSES TO A ROBIN REDBREAST

WHO VISITS THE WINDOW OF MY PRISON EVERY DAY

Welcome, pretty little stranger—
  Welcome to my lone retreat;
Here, secure from every danger,
  Hop about and chirp and eat.
    Robin! how I envy thee,
    Happy bird of liberty.

Now, though tyrant Winter howling
  Shakes the world with tempest round,
Heaven above with vapours scowling,
  Frost imprisons all the ground.
    Robin! what are these to thee—
    Thou art blest with liberty.

Though yon fair majestic river[130]
  Mourns in solid icy chains;
Though yon flocks and cattle shiver
  On the desolated plains—
    Robin! thou art gay and free,
    Happy in thy liberty.

Hunger never shall distress thee
  While my cates[131] one crumb affords;
Colds or cramps shall ne'er oppress thee,
  Come and share my humble board.
    Robin! come and live with me,
    Live, yet still at liberty.

Soon shall Spring in smiles and blushes
  Steal upon the blooming year;
Then amid th'enamour'd bushes

---

[130] The Ouse.

[131] Delicious food. Prison diet was not very delicate.

Thy sweet song shall warble clear;
   Then shall I, too, join with thee,
   Swell the hymn of liberty.

Should some rough unfeeling Dobbin,
  In this iron-hearted age,
Seize thee on thy nest, my Robin,
  And confine thee in a cage:
   Then, poor prisoner! think of me,
   Think and sigh for liberty.

Liberty's[132] the brightest jewel
  In the crown of earthly joys:
All sensations else are cruel,
  All delights besides are toys.
   None but captives such as me
   Know the worth of liberty.

THE FUNERAL

"And who can grieve too much; what time shall end
Our mourning for so dear a friend?"   CREECH.

I'll tell you what happened of late,
At old Roger Cockayne's interment;
He'd long been apprised of his fate,[133]

---

[132] This verse is omitted in Montgomery's collected works. It may be on account of its grammatical construction: it certainly cannot be on account of the sentiments it contains. The intrinsic beauty of the piece will ever make it a favourite with the public; but an additional interest attaches to it if we consider the occasion on which it was written. Montgomery was undergoing his three months' imprisonment, in York Castle, for publishing a "Patriotic Song" written by a clergyman. It would require no stretch of imagination to picture the solitary bard viewing "poor robin" with the most ardent solicitude, and perhaps, like Sterne's startling, exclaiming, "*I can't get out.*"

[133] "With Ancus and Numa, Kings of Rome,
   We must descend into the silent tomb." SPETT.

Was a man of some little discernment;
By relatives distant and near
Roger's death had been anticipated,[134]
His money was what they held dear,
So they came to see things regulated.

Jerry Selby and Tamar came first,
His first wife was Roger's own sister;
He was uncle to young Jossy Hurst,
And brother to Barbara Lister[135]
Anthony Kay's second wife
And Roger were both by a mother;[136]
There was nought but contention and strife
For one wanted more than another.

Leonard Scargill arrived, unexpected,
With Sally behind him from Tickhill:
The mourners seem'd greatly affected,
And Barbara took hold of Mickel;
In Bradfield their ancestors lies,[137]
From Worrall the funeral started:
If a tear chanced to drop from their eyes,
It was not for their brother departed.

Tears, say a writer of merit,

---

[134] It is thought by the author that Roger's friends had constantly in view what was so beautifully expressed by Antiphanes, a very ancient poet, who lived a hundred years before Socrates. "Be not grieved," said he, "for thy deceased friends; they are not dead, but have only finished that journey which it is necessary for every one of us to take."

[135] See Mapplebeck's Letters—letter 3,007.

[136] John Smith humourously introduces Roger's relatives in this song. Hunter, the historian, in his copy of Smith's songs, has drawn the genealogy of the Cockayne family. The volume is now in the library of John Guest, Esq., Rotherham.

[137] See Lloyd's Worthies, and the Author's Genealogical History, 3rd edt., vol. 5th, p. 28.

Are oft shed from different causes;[138]
They'll spring from a turbulent spirit,
Yet sometimes real sorrow discloses;
When from the grave they return'd,
And sorrow and grief had subsided,
Each with anxiety burned
To know how the cash was divided.

Michael read with an audible voice,
Which some heard with seeming composure:
Give Jerry the five acre cloise,
And Michael the upper enclosure;
Give Jossy the Loxley estate,[139]
And Leonard the homestead and dairy;
Give Nelly the old pewter plate,[140]
And the chest made i'th'reign o' Queen Mary.

The house now resounded with curses,
For Nelly gave vent to her feelings;
You're some of you lining your purses,
Ye gods, what unmerciful dealings;
The mourners seemed buried in thought,
Afraid of the talons of Nelly;
She wished he'd the plate in his throat,
And his old-fashioned chest in his belly.

They saw Nelly's passion was rising,
So did what they could to appease her;
But what appeared most surprising,
It took three o'th strongest to seize her!
This made her more aggravated,

---

[138] Vide Young's Night Thoughts.

[139] Mapplebeck's Ancient Tenures, vol. 9th. p. 97, 8vo., 2nd edt.

[140] For the importance attached to bequests of this kind, see Sir Everard Digbye's Will, 1508: "I bequeath to my sonne, Everard Digbye, my grettest brass pot, to be kept for a standard of that house, and the next brass pot and two little brass pottes and half a garnish of pewter vessels, and all tubbys and bolles within my house."

Hoods and scarfs were promiscuously blended,
'Twas high time they all separated,
They did!—and the tumult was ended.

ROTHERHAM STATUTES[141]

"Who better seen than I, in shepherds' arts,
To please the lads and win the lasses' hearts?
For many songs and tales of mirth had I."   PHILIPS.

Sam Firth to Rotherham statutes went
  With Grace from Birley-moor,
With Rachel Stones and Esther Dent,
  Who ne'er had been before;
"Where now?" cried Jonas Bradbury,
  Sam happened to turn his back;
Lid Grub and Dinah Dewsbury
  Roll'd up[142] wi' Jacob Slack.

They merrily jogg'd it on apace,
  Until they came to th' town:
"Some puts up at th' Cranes," says Grace,
  "But I'll put up at th' Crown;"
Grace' cheeks were red, her eyes were black,
  So tight was every rag;
Sam's soles were near two inches thick,
  With here and there a brag.
Math Birks and Tet had took their place
  With Mat from Nether Green;
Gin Walsh and Fan stood next to Grace,

---

[141] This song was written about 1804, and celebrates the doings at Rotherham statutes. John Smith, the author, has well described the manner in which the evenings were spent at the statutes." The description of the dancing is very racy.

[142] "Roll'd up" is a genuine Sheffield expression for people assembling. I remember a *learned* native once translating the phrase thus: "The folks begin to conglomerate rare and fast."

Goff Thompson stood between;
Jonathan Crookes was th' first to bid,
   He stared 'em fair i' th' face;
He felt at Mat, and handled Lid,
   But fix'd his mind on Grace.

Now Grace to go seem'd very loth,
   And leave Sam Firth behind;
Says Jonathan Crookes, "I'll hire you both,
   But not against your mind;
Sep Merrill knows well what beast I keep,
   I've forty acres of land,
Three mares and a horse, and twenty sheep,
   And I live at Wooburn Stand."[143]

Then Goff and Sam, and Grace and Mat,
   Took right away to th' Crown:
Jont Shaw and Deborah Frost were sat,
   Kit Lidget and Zanker Brown;
The fiddler sang so sweet and clear,
   He far excell'd the lark;
He played 'em "Farewell, Manchester,"
   And warbled until dark.

When night came on the game begun,
   They drank hot ale and gin;
Grace's face was like the rising sun,
   And Sam felt warm within;
When they'd paid, and took their place,
   The fiddler soon struck off:
Sam cross'd o'er a couple with Grace,
   And Mat led through wi' Goff.

Sam set to Dinah Dewsbury,
   Then reel'd about with Sall;
He singled with Jonas Bradbury,

---

[143] From the ancient Saxon of Hoober, or Hooburgh. See Scorah's Travels, vol. 3, p.187 to 193.

Then set again to Nell;
He then flew up the middle,
And reel'd about with Kit;
His *pumps* just touch'd the fiddle,
And smash'd it bit from bit.[144]

Sam stared—his hair stood quite erect,
And Grace's sun went down;
Goff Thompson says, "We must collect,"
And so said Zanker Brown;
Sam tipp'd Goff two shillings in hand—
He'll mind better for time to come!
They both took off to Wooburn Stand,
To dance where there's more room!

---

[144] This verse finely describes a "penny hop." Sam's "pumps" smashing the fiddle was not to be wondered at seeing his soles were two inches thick. Before the opening of the railway it was curious to watch the departure of the old "Waterloo" from Waingate "to't stattis" with those who mingled in the "stirrings" at these annual hirings.

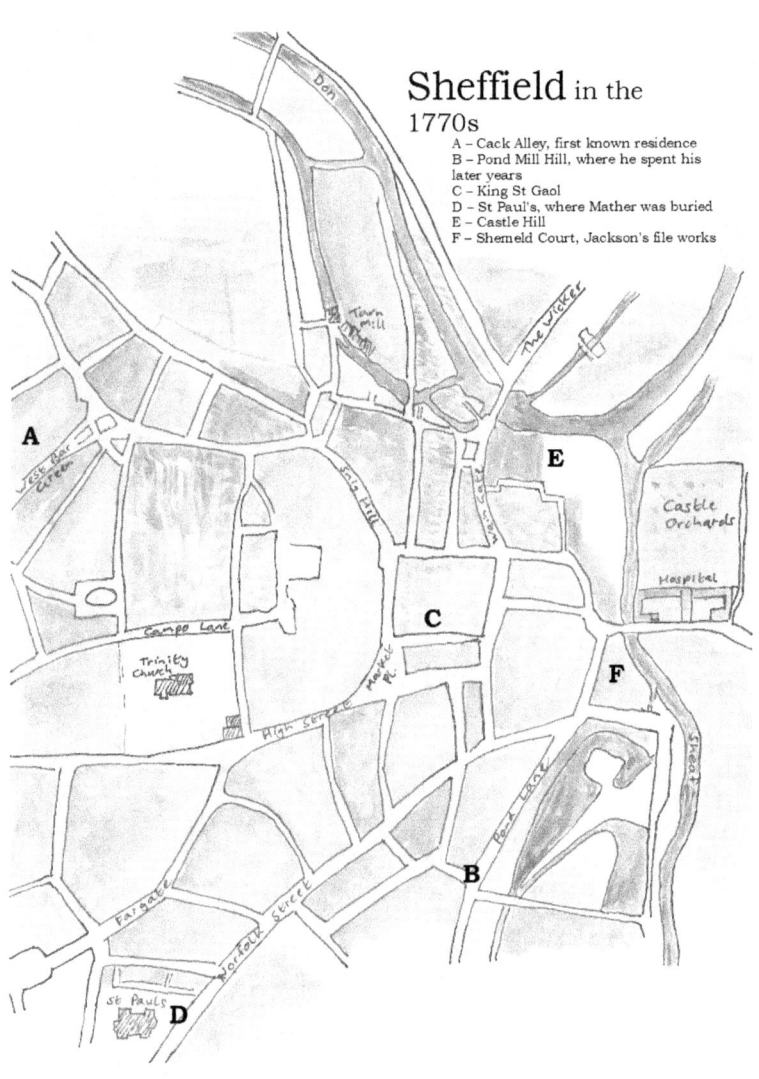

Memorial marking the spot at Abbey Lane Cemetery where remains from St Paul's were re-interred.

www.ingramcontent.com/pod-product-compliance
Lightning Source LLC
Chambersburg PA
CBHW070611300426
44113CB00010B/1495